Editorial correspondence:
Rhonda Bailey, Editorial Director
XYZ Publishing
P.O. Box 250
Lantzville BC
V0R 2H0
E-mail: xyzed@shaw.ca

In the same collection

Ven Begamudré, *Isaac Brock: Larger Than Life.*

Lynne Bowen, *Robert Dunsmuir: Laird of the Mines.*

Kate Braid, *Emily Carr: Rebel Artist.*

Kathryn Bridge, *Phyllis Munday: Mountaineer.*

William Chalmers, *George Mercer Dawson: Geologist, Scientist, Explorer.*

Judith Fitzgerald, *Marshall McLuhan: Wise Guy.*

lian goodall, *William Lyon Mackenzie King: Dreams and Shadows.*

Stephen Eaton Hume, *Frederick Banting: Hero, Healer, Artist.*

Naïm Kattan, *A.M. Klein: Poet and Prophet.*

Betty Keller, *Pauline Johnson: First Aboriginal Voice of Canada.*

Michelle Labrèche-Larouche, *Emma Albani: International Star.*

Wayne Larsen, *A.Y. Jackson: A Love for the Land.*

Francine Legaré, *Samuel de Champlain: Father of New France.*

Margaret Macpherson, *Nellie McClung: Voice for the Voiceless.*

Dave Margoshes, *Tommy Douglas: Building the New Society.*

Marguerite Paulin, *René Lévesque: Charismatic Leader.*

Raymond Plante, *Jacques Plante: Behind the Mask.*

T.F. Rigelhof, *George Grant: Redefining Canada.*

Arthur Slade, *John Diefenbaker: An Appointment with Destiny.*

Roderick Stewart, *Wilfrid Laurier: A Pledge for Canada.*

John Wilson, *John Franklin: Traveller on Undiscovered Seas.*

John Wilson, *Norman Bethune: A Life of Passionate Conviction.*

Rachel Wyatt, *Agnes Macphail: Champion of the Underdog.*

John Grierson

National Library of Canada Cataloguing in Publication

Evans, Gary, 1944-

    John Grierson : trailblazer of documentary film

    (The Quest library ; 24)

    Includes bibliographical references and index.

    ISBN 1-894852-15-X

    1. Grierson, John, 1898-1972. 2. National Film Board of Canada - History. 3. Documentary films - Canada - History and criticism. 4. Motion picture producers and directors - Canada - Biography. I. Title. II. Series: Quest library ; 24.

PN1998.3.G75E92 2005   791.4302'32'092   C2005-940219-9

Legal Deposit: First quarter 2005
National Library of Canada
Bibliothèque nationale du Québec

XYZ Publishing acknowledges the support of The Quest Library project by the Canadian Studies Program and the Book Publishing Industry Development Program (BPIDP) of the Department of Canadian Heritage. The opinions expressed do not necessarily reflect the views of the Government of Canada.

The publishers further acknowledge the financial support our publishing program receives from The Canada Council for the Arts, the ministère de la Culture et des Communications du Québec, and the Société de développement des entreprises culturelles.

Chronology: Gary Evans
Index: Darcy Dunton
Layout: Édiscript enr.
Cover design: Zirval Design
Cover illustration: Magali Lefrançois
Photo research: Gary Evans and NFB Photothèque staff
Photos used with permission of the National Film Board of Canada

Printed and bound in Canada

XYZ Publishing
1781 Saint Hubert Street
Montreal, Quebec H2L 3Z1
Tel: (514) 525-2170
Fax: (514) 525-7537
E-mail: info@xyzedit.qc.ca
Web site: www.xyzedit.qc.ca

Distributed by: Fitzhenry & Whiteside
195 Allstate Parkway
Markham, ON L3R 4T8
Customer Service, tel: (905) 477-9700
Toll free ordering, tel: 1-800-387-9776
Fax: 1-800-260-9777
E-mail: bookinfo@fitzhenry.ca

International Rights: Contact André Vanasse, tel. (514) 525-2170 # 25
E-mail: andre.vanasse@xyzedit.qc.ca

GRIERSON

John

TRAILBLAZER OF DOCUMENTARY FILM

XYZ
Publishing

For Karin

Contents

During the Second World War, John Grierson explains
propaganda to a National Film Board artist, "Selling the war
is not like selling corn flakes. Sometimes you have
to make people believe what they ought to believe
rather than what they want to believe."

Prologue

Who Was That Man?

The young editor has been waiting nervously over an hour for his boss to see his finished film. He hopes the newsreel can be released by deadline, the end of November, 1941. Suddenly the studio door is kicked open and in rushes a short, mustachioed, energized blur, with blazing blue eyes that look hawk-like around the theatre. Spotting the editor, the boss bellows, "Well, what the hell are you waiting for? Roll it!" He lights a cigarette. He reminds the editor of the Edward G. Robinson character in *Little Caesar*. His fierce look could kill.

Twenty minutes and two cigarettes later, the film ends and the boss wheels about in his seat. His Scots accent cuts through the darkness. "What did God Almighty give you for brains? It's not about bravado and how we're ready for war, it's about winning the U.S. public and getting them into the war. Now go back and recut the conclusion. We want the Big Picture, the Big Picture, dammit! The Japanese navy is powerful and ready to hit somewhere in the Pacific. Tell the truth. We're in for some sticky times." He leaps to his feet and races out of the theatre, leaving only the pall of blue tobacco smoke.

The young Canadian editor is crestfallen. His director comforts him in his cool, composed Cambridge English accent. "We're almost there. He liked it, because he only wants the conclusion recut. We'll make the deadline. Let's get going."

∞

They recut the film's ending just as the boss had dictated. *Warclouds in the Pacific* opened in Canada and the U.S. a week later, and days afterward, the Japanese navy attacked Pearl Harbor. America was finally at war. Many wondered how this Canadian newsreel *seemed to know* the Japanese had some terrible plans for the Pacific and pointed to Pearl Harbor one week before the sneak attack happened!

Soon after, a bevy of lawyers from Time-Life Incorporated launched a lawsuit against this Canadian film. Before long, the volcanic little man with the piercing blue eyes was in New York in a faceoff. The Americans argued that they could stop *Warclouds in the Pacific* because their own series, *The March of*

Time, had loaned the Canadians some stock shots of ships. The real reason they meant to stop its distribution was that the Canadians had scooped them. The Americans wanted their own newsreel to announce the Japanese threat.

The legal men in suits had heard through the grapevine that this Scots Napoleon had staged one grandstand play when he called *The March of Time* representative into his office and grabbed his phone – "Get me the Prime Minister's Office, NOW! Tell him it's Grierson at the National Film Board."

While waiting he lit a cigarette, hoisted his feet up on his desk, crossed them, and pointed with his cigarette, "Now we in Canada are barely mentioned at all in the thirteen issues you Yanks produce a year. There is room enough in the North American market for films on editorial war reporting. Let's have our personal considerations align with the larger issues. In short, let's work together. We'll give a screen credit to you folks, but the film stands as it is." The representative was sufficiently frightened at the possibility of the Prime Minister's Office being involved to say he would recommend this course to his New York legal minions. "Okay then," the gruff character conceded. "Cancel that call to the PM's Office," he bellowed into the phone. He swung his feet off the desk, brushed his hand against his lips, and smiled. "Let's go have a drink." Grabbing his black fedora, he thought the battle was over.

But the New York newsreel people would not budge. The next thing they knew, the fiery Scotsman was in Manhattan standing before them and the legal minions of Time-Life Incorporated. "Gentleman, I have tried to accommodate you but it is clear that no concession is sufficiently to your liking. I have it from the highest authority in Canada that if *The March of Time* insists on pressing this lawsuit, Canada will revise the existing laws regarding the importation of foreign films into Canada." A number of men around the table blanched white. There was silence for a moment, then one attorney spoke to his angry boss, whose face, unlike the others, was flushing red. "You started something you can't finish. Drop it." The silence was profound. Everyone knew at that instant the lawsuit was over.

John Grierson implied that his direct line to the Prime Minister's Office was sufficient authority for him to have made this statement. No one was ready to call his bluff and jeopardize what Hollywood insisted (and insists to this day) was part of their domestic market. *Warclouds in the Pacific* received nationwide distribution in the United States. The film put Canada on the map for hundreds of thousands of Americans, and began the regular showing of Film Board shorts in the U.S. until the war ended.

How did this man in motion know about Japan's plans? Was it coincidence? Probably. "It was simply a matter of geopolitics," he admitted three decades later. "The Germans were at the gates of Moscow and the Japanese knew it was now or never to get the drop on the Yanks. Simple geopolitics."

Who was this man? And why was a Scotsman telling Canadians what to do while being cozy with the prime minister of Canada? His name was John

Grierson, and as founder of the documentary film movement in Britain and the National Film Board of Canada (NFB), he was in an unparalleled position of power and influence when it came to film in Canada. He, who had invented the word "documentary," was called upon by Prime Minister Mackenzie King in 1939 to head Canada's National Film Board and to supervise the distribution of wartime information to the free press and radio. The newpapers called him Canada's Propaganda Maestro. His authoritarian personality put some people off. Others understood his posturing. He put a ring of steel around young filmmakers while ensuring that the newsreels they were making were serving the greatest cause of all: democracy.

This Scotsman's contribution to Canada and Canadian communications was profound, not just during the Second World War, but also years afterwards, when he returned to Canada to teach at McGill University in Montreal and where he advised the Canadian Radio and Television Commission in Ottawa about the best path to follow in the dawning world of global electronic communication, what Marshall McLuhan was calling in 1968 "the global village." From his earliest years, Grierson understood the dawning new world. He became a visionary who preached that effective mass communication could enrich individual lives and perhaps even end humans' tendency to kill off each other in war. That message, in the form of moving images in a brand new medium, became his life's work.

As a child sitting in a chilly classroom in Scotland, Grierson was thrilled by the magic of movies as a clanking battery-operated projector illuminated the natural wonders of Canada.

1

White Magic

Born two years before the new century, John Grierson grew up in a village school not far from Glasgow in a Scottish family that both thrived on discipline and loved education and debate. They practised Calvinism, a dour Protestant doctrine that preached the virtues of hard work, education, thrift, good deeds, and unwavering faith that God had chosen them for heavenly salvation. It was not easy to be heard as one of eight children, especially as John and his younger brother Anthony were perched in the middle, the only males. His father Robert ran the school.

At the tender age of six, John sat in the unheated classroom near a large battery-operated machine called a projector, which was throwing its brilliant white light against the bare wall. A projectionist threaded a reel of celluloid through an opening at the top. Suddenly the contraption began to clack noisily and then a moving image appeared. For thirty seconds, a child ate his breakfast cereal. The projectionist repeated the procedure and there appeared a train winding through a river valley that was carpeted on both sides with huge pine trees. Over the mechanical din his father spoke to the class, "This is the Fraser River Valley in the province of British Columbia in the Dominion of Canada. This province has more trees than three United Kingdoms put together and its entire population is less than Glasgow's. Canada has a single railway linking the Atlantic to the Pacific."

Grierson was fascinated by his first film show. His father, a progressive Presbyterian, ignored those who called film black magic and the work of the Devil. He had introduced film to the school as education, not as sinful entertainment. Film was "white magic" that observed actuality, opened a window on the world, illuminated and educated. John became an instant convert to the new medium.

Both parents were strict, but caring. Robert was a quiet, conservative, unsmiling man whose keen blue eyes brightened when he talked about the Grierson heritage and Scotland. "Always be proud of our family. Lighthouses are in our blood, son. Griersons were lighthouse keepers in the Inner Hebrides, perched on the wild rocks and promontories of the Highland seas. A Grierson even helped build the Bell Rock light on the North Sea. And I, as a teacher, continue the job of illuminating, only now it is to enlighten young minds."

His mother Jane, also a teacher, sparked John's lifelong interest in politics and public service. She was a fiercely vocal independent thinker and suffragette who came from a long radical tradition. She also ran a soup kitchen in the village. Dependent as it was on the cotton mills alongside the River Teith as well as the mines nearby, the village suffered periodic economic depressions. John once ran crying to his mother after some boys, mocking those on welfare, teased him about the poor having to drink her soup that was peppered with beetles. "That will teach you about how hard it is to be a socialist," she retorted. "Stop your snivelling and help me carry this pot." It was his first political lesson. It did no good to cry over those who mocked the unemployed workers' despair, poverty, and dependency. His mother was teaching John to take social responsibility. They carried her soup to the hungry Scots villagers. He now understood what it was to grow up in a small, dependent country that was part of the unsympathetic capitalist world.

∽

At age ten, John began high school, an intense workout in Calvinist discipline. The typical eight-hour school day was followed by soccer, dinner, and homework from 6:30 till midnight. He was of slight build, and his sandy hair made his light blue eyes stand out luminously. His voice developed into a combination of rich Scots burr and classical English. It deepened to a perfect baritone that sounded commanding, no matter what he said. That voice helped make him a natural leader. John excelled in school and yet did not show off in class. He impressed people when he was called upon to speak, and teachers observed that he had a natural gift that propelled him to effortless superiority. Finishing high school in 1915, he won a four-year university scholarship. The First World War had been raging for a year, and like millions in Great Britain, John was convinced the world would never be the same again. Adding two years to his age, he volunteered for the Royal Navy.

He wrote to his family how the experience of serving as a wireless operator on a North Sea minesweeper was a sobering passage to adulthood. "I have watched men blown to Kingdom Come and shot to pieces by enemy submarines," he said. "To keep my sanity, I spend four hours a day reading and writing. I have mastered Italian, philosophy, and French literature. I am quite the cosmopolitan Scotsman." It was good discipline, since by the time he was demobilized three years later, Grierson had completed his first year of university. He had also developed a conviction that peace must be made more exciting than war.

Postwar, he found it difficult to fit in at the University of Glasgow, which seethed with the froth of conservative, liberal, and socialist ferment. The university custom was to teach students to debate issues from those three prevailing political positions. This was good practice to develop his own analytical thinking, yet he wrote to his parents angrily, "I hate my professors who seem oblivious to the moral dilemma of the Great War and its 37 million casualties. The real issue is, 'Can future wars be prevented?'" The surly young veteran refused to take lecture notes that first year. Old politics had failed, and like many men of his generation, he was drawn to socialism. He liked being left wing without committing himself to a specific party.

Grierson was recognizable instantly as he rolled across campus with the sailor's gait he had developed in the navy. The short, now mustachioed undergraduate sported a bowler hat and oversized military trench coat slapping his ankles, Charlie Chaplin style. He could even have passed for the comic genius, whose films he reviewed in the university's literary magazine.

After joining the socialist Fabian Society, Grierson usually arrived late to meetings, greeted no one, hoisted his feet up to the fire, and pretended to sleep while others spoke. At last, he seemed to wake up suddenly. He stuffed his pipe with tobacco, lit it with a firebrand from the hearth, and fixed his light blue eyes on something or someone as he began his oration. "Now see here. Once the common people understand their relationship to each other and to the world around them, they will achieve progressive social democratic change. BY THEMSELVES. They need not follow the path of socialism nor must they depend on the emergence of a powerful state. It is there for them to grasp by themselves."

A few of the shocked listeners scoffed and called him a humbug. This was not socialism, but mystical utopian idealism, a kind of top-down philosophy of communication. Grierson did not flinch. Not then, not ever. He devastated fellow students with his biting arguments and verbal ability and was such a formidable debater that his racy speech, analytical penetration, and thrusting logic often left them stunned, exhilarated, and angry. He had one weakness: He could not listen.

And if he overwhelmed his audience with fact, figure, and philosophy, he also enjoyed playing with fire another way: Grierson loved struggling with contradictory opposites. His Calvinist Presbyterian roots and thorough knowledge of the Bible qualified him to preach in church. One Sunday, he started out traditionally and with much success: "Each of us must take our part establishing good things, before good things can come to pass... It is for each of us to live and to live strongly for the community of men, and to act according to the light that is in us..." Emboldened by success, at another service he claimed, "I condemn communist politics like any right thinking God-fearing Christian. But we should admire Lenin and Trotsky for both the social experiment being tried in Russia and the new release of human energies." There was nearly a riot in church as parishioners howled at such a radical sermon. They booed him off the pulpit. Defrocked, he never spoke in a church again. Pushing to the limit was Grierson's Achilles' heel. He thought it fun to be outrageous and confidently careless.

∞

After receiving his master's degree, Grierson began teaching college in northern England at Newcastle upon Tyne. The local slums featured endless dreary smoke-stained identical brick row houses, street after street, whose only distinction was the colour and state of the peeling paint on the front doors and the amount of horse manure on the cobblestones before them. His class, made up of tired old clerks and spinsters there to learn Plato, wanted to ignore the town's horrid industrial working conditions, the malnourished children, and schools that seemed like prisons. The new teacher faced an uphill climb as half the class dozed, one-quarter of their faces showed as much interest as a flat sea, and the rest either scribbled fiercely or doodled in their notebooks. Grierson struggled to get them to speak.

Once, he tried to explain Plato's Allegory of the Cave. "Imagine prisoners chained immobile inside a cave. Real objects are being carried past a huge bonfire behind them; they can see only the objects' shadows on the wall before them. One day a prisoner is freed. In the sunshine he sees the objects as they really are. Enlightened, he returns to free his comrades but they reject him. Why? Because having been in the sunlight, he can no longer identify the shadows and shapes they call reality until his eyes become used to the dark again. The allegory is clear: people are unable to see reality without the illumination of thought and reason. And those who have seen truth must struggle to convince others."

"Any questions?" Silence. At last a timid hand went halfway up. "Will this be on the final exam, Sir?" Defeat. He wondered, "Am I reaching them at all?" He remembered his promise to his mother that, like her, he would try to ease the suffering of the unfortunate.

But sometimes in the dark of his unheated cold-water flat, he stared through an unwashed window into the night and like so many others before and after, wondered if this was all there was after graduation. Would he spend the rest of his life as a cipher in a forgotten town in a forgotten country?

He shook off doubt and wrote home, "If schools and churches have already lost their power to move the masses, it is popular media that are taking their place. I think my nose for the future is unerring. I must find out more about how mass communications are shaping public opinion." With his degree and a Rockefeller fellowship under his arm, he set off for Chicago in 1924.

2

Itinerant Journalist in America

A fter the United States outlawed alcohol sales in 1919, criminals thrived on its illegal sale, especially in Chicago, where Al Capone was bootleg king. Grierson, terrified and thrilled, was shocked at the violence and mayhem he found there in 1924. He lived in a tiny room on the North side, close to the O'Banion flower shop where a hapless gangster, whose name sounded Irish, met his end in a hail of machine-gun fire. "He may have been a poor hood, but they buried the palooka in a $10,000 casket," he remarked with stylized gangster rhetoric to his new friends, a bohemian couple named Rudolph and Fritzie Weisenborn. He became caught up in their excitement

In the 1920s, the young, energetic, and enthusiastic journalist decided after meeting Hollywood's stars that film should better be used for educational purposes. He would call it documentary film.

with the visual dynamics of a city whose architecture was clambering outward and upward, catching light in a thousand new ways. Other lights drew them too. He made a bargain: "I'll furnish the booze and pay for movie and theatre tickets if you feed me."

He thrived as they introduced him to speakeasies, art world friends, and to the jazz of little-known musicians like Louis Armstrong and Bessie Smith. Rudolph, a painter, taught Grierson how to better use his eyes to analyse film, and the two fought over movies like brothers. Grierson had a tender spot for Rudolph's wife Fritzie, who played referee, and the three were seen constantly around Chicago's bustling art scene.

Grierson probably never intended to earn a degree at the University of Chicago, but he was interested in mass communications as taught by political scientist Charles Merriman, sociologist Robert Park, and media effects scholar Harold Lasswell. Viewing the melting pot process was the most important part of his Chicago experience, and he planned to study how immigrants were integrated into American society. Looking at Skid Row dropouts, he found that many had tried and failed to integrate and had turned their backs on their Old World parents.

He became a newspapers junkie, reading four a day. His single room quickly filled with newsprint and once, as Fritzie stopped by to patch up the latest quarrel between John and her husband, she found nowhere to sit. She looked around. His bed, a war-surplus cot with no mattress, was rumpled, its lightweight green blanket strewn with the day's press and stained by newsprint. A wardrobe door was open, revealing two suit jackets and two pairs of pants, none of which matched. A box of freshly done laundry was open and she counted four pressed shirts. His table and chair were stacked with books and magazines and topped by both empty and full cigarette packages. A cup of cold coffee stood next to an electric hotplate; it looked half-evaporated and gave off a stale odour. An ashtray filled with butts was perched on the single window ledge; the frame, which had been painted shut years ago, kept out the wicked Chicago wind as well as the now fresh spring air. The air was blue with smoke from his ever-lit cigarette. Only a single poster hung on the wall opposite his cot. He had designed it himself as an incentive to get out of bed and get moving: It read, Eventually – Why Not Now?

Fritzie leaned against the wall. Grierson ignored her inability to find a place to sit and paced feverishly, talking and gesturing nonstop. "Why, I wonder, in spite of six thousand foreign-language papers, is the Hearst press dominant? Because the Hearst press is sensationalist. It has positioned itself primitively and dramatically. Its daily headlines scream at you and demonstrate the importance of the active verb: 'Someone does something to someone,' or 'Something happens to someone.'" He pointed to a murder story headline. "Don't you see? No bleeding hearts. Sentimentality only pleases our nostalgia for a different world, but reveals nothing about this one. The Hearst technique is so simple: a report must become a story that holds facts together in a living organic relationship." He carried on as excitedly as if he had discovered gold. Bemused at this Scots fireball, Fritzie smiled and chortled, "Well, aren't you the active verb, John? If you were a candle, you would be a pool of wax."

Grierson ignored her comment and said he wanted to apply this strategy of being dramatically active. He soon honed his skills writing a newspaper column about painting for the *Evening Post* as well as doing film reviews for *The Chicagoan*. Later, he applied the same technique in designing the structure of documentary film.

In 1925 he met Walter Lippmann, the author of the renowned book, *Public Opinion*. Lippmann, a conservative whose loyalties were on behalf of the moneyed and powerful interests who employed him, had written that democracy was no longer workable in a busy society where individuals were cut off from learning about events happening around them. Nor were they able to make informed decisions. With so many facts to know and too little time to learn them, it was up to the educated elite, and not the masses, to lead and make decisions. Later media theorists described this elite as "manufacturing the consent" of the general population.

At a speakeasy with the Weisenborns one night, Grierson scowled at Lippmann's antidemocratic ideas while Louis Armstrong played in the background. "Why won't he encourage the educated elite to *listen* to the public, and then educate the masses about how democracy could work?" he asked. "The masses need these elites to say what they cannot express, but can *feel*. If Lippmann weren't so busy being famous and in thrall to the boys with all the money, he might have come up with a better suggestion for me to measure how society itself is changing."

"What did he say?" asked Rudolph. "Study the impact of film," Grierson replied glumly. They nursed drinks quietly as Armstrong broke into song, "Up a lazy river by the old mill stream..." Then Grierson bolted upright as if struck. "You know, after all, he's right. What is popular at the box office reflects public taste. And the best way to do this," he concluded excitedly, "is to investigate movie ticket sales." A big smile crossed his face. He had found his project.

Weeks later, an enthusiastic Grierson was in Hollywood studying studio statistics of Paramount Pictures. Walter Wanger invited him to watch films being produced and to join him at the Brown Derby on Hollywood Boulevard. Arriving late and dressed indifferently, Grierson marvelled at the limousines that were parked outside: a canary yellow Stutz Bearcat, a gun barrel blue Mercedes Maybach, and a white convertible Duesenberg, whose hood was longer than the rest of the car. He entered and was about to be thrown out by the maitre d' when Wanger called out, "That's okay, Clifton, he's with us." Grierson could hardly believe his eyes. Here was the great Charlie Chaplin, fresh from filming *The Gold Rush*. He was laughing about how thirty takes of the shoe-and-lace-eating scene had made his co-star sick from eating so much licorice. Grierson commented that as a film critic for his university magazine, he had praised Chaplin's films for showing the twentieth-century "little man" with sympathy.

Chaplin's clipped English accent sounded strange coming from the screen image that never spoke. "Really?" He asked earnestly. "How very kind of you. I always saw the Tramp as myself down and out, before I stumbled onto success. Why don't you come over to my place next Friday? I'm having a party for newspapermen and young starlets. The champagne is a gift from the gods." Grierson went and learned how the great Chaplin practised the first rule of staying in the public's eye: Befriend the critics. Chaplin moved from one to another, telling each confidentially that *The Gold Rush* would be his best film ever. They obliged him in print. Publicity, short, sweet and to the point, is what manipulating mass media was all about. It was a lesson Grierson kept for the rest of his life.

Later, Grierson met celebrities Joseph Von Sternberg, Erich von Stroheim, F.W. Murnau, King Vidor, and Ernst Lubitsch. They did not know what to make of this energetic Scotsman who, ignoring his sandwich but never his cigarette, talked about how Hollywood stars' rise and fall reflected changing public taste, pretension, and achievement. His mouth and body never stopped moving.

Meeting the stars did not blind Grierson, though he did appreciate these artists whose films he thought were provoking social change. But in a series of articles for *Motion Picture* News, he called Hollywood films shabby as a whole. "The film industry despises their audience in the name of profit," he complained. "Cinema belongs to the mob. It is the only genuine democratic institution that has ever appeared on a worldwide scale. If movies touch the greatest number of people with the democratic ideal, why are they doing so little to interpret the contemporary world?" Grierson concluded that Hollywood's talented artists were too interested in themselves and getting rich to make cinema great. Hollywood, movie stars, and glitz would never support the kind of movie he was thinking about.

∞

He had left dirt on the carpet on his California trip, but this was characteristically Grierson. He returned to journalism in New York City, where he wrote for the *New York Sun* and held forth at his favourite watering hole, the Coffee House Club. He enjoyed outraging conservatives as he praised recent Soviet films, especially Sergei Eisenstein's 1925 masterpiece *Battleship Potemkin*, whose themes of brotherhood and an end to class divisions had led authorities in Britain, France, and Germany to censor and/or ban it. "If a film has visual rhythm in presenting objective social reality, it achieves psychological connection," he explained to one staid wag who protested Eisenstein's film was communist subversion. Grierson took this personally. "Open your eyes and see its greatest moment, the Odessa steps sequence. Three hundred non-actors, choreographed to create a vast movement, a building of tempo. See the violent use of editing for smash effects and symbolic counterpoint. You see," he continued, voice rising, "Eisenstein was first to make it plain that film could be an adult and positive *illuminating* force in the world. The Russians have learned to use art as a hammer. They are far ahead of the West."

The straitlaced listener stiffened, "A sales talk is a sales talk. It is communist subversion and you, sir, are pandering to it. Disgusting." He rose quickly and bumped the man at the next table, knocking over his coffee. He stormed out.

At that table, wiping his saturated shirt, sat a morose-looking hulk of a man in a crumpled white linen suit and panama hat, the kind of outfit usually worn in the tropics. He slugged back what remained of his "coffee," came over to Grierson, shook hands limply, and mumbled, "You'll never be as Catholic as the Pope. I'm Bob Flaherty." The great American explorer and poet of cinema, Robert Flaherty, sat down. The two shared their flasks of illegal gin. The longer they refilled each other's coffee cups, the more articulate their conversation became.

Grierson recalled seeing Flaherty's immortal 1922 silent classic, *Nanook of the North*, the story of an Inuit family's hunt for food in the Canadian North. Lubricated by the alcohol and his own enthusiasm, Grierson declared, "I liked the poetry of your exploratory style and the way its tempo spelled out a drama that resides in living fact." Flaherty was flattered but depressed. Paramount had just tied up his new film, *Moana*, shot in British Samoa, and wanted to re-edit it to emphasize the sexiness of the topless natives. They insisted on calling it "The Love-Life of a South Sea Siren" in posters and ads. Deep into his cups, Flaherty asked, "What in hell's name am I going to do to save it?"

Grierson said he would try to help. They campaigned vigorously in print for the film's special promotion and filled theatres in six test city locations. Most importantly, the day after the film opened, Grierson wrote effusively in the *Sun*. "*Moana* is great," he enthused, "And deserves to rank with those few works of the screen that have the right to last, to live. It has documentary value... but it is beautiful... and achieves greatness through its poetic feeling for natural elements... It is lovely beyond compare... A flame shot up, kindled light and the art form had been added to observation."

Flaherty's work had inspired Grierson to introduce the word "documentary" into English film language. The French had used the word to describe travel or exploration films, but Grierson would attach it to the movement he was about to start. The world of film would never be the same as the Scotsman used a branding iron to imprint the definition, which remains to this day. He admitted later, "It is a clumsy description, but let it stand: Documentary is the creative interpretation of actuality."

The two men became great drinking pals and over two decades they consumed untold quantities of alcohol "in a pub crawl over half the world." Eyeing his friend through his glass, Grierson insisted on film containing naturalism within a social and political context. "I love your poetic genius, Bob," he said, finishing an argument typically with the last word. "You go do the savages at the end of the earth and I'll do the savages in Birmingham." This Scots rapscallion was not easy to love. He did not care. He was having the time of his life.

Grierson's Rockefeller fellowship ended. He had stopped attending university, had not finished his research project or degree, and had become an itinerant journalist in America. He left the U.S. in 1927, having gained another sort of education. Mentally, he was already building upon Flaherty's exploratory style and was fixed on a goal of using film to illuminate "drama that resides in living fact." The film art of Eisenstein and Flaherty had taught him that struggle was inherently dramatic and beautiful if it was social, not individual. Now back to Britain to find it.

National Film Board of Canada.

While shooting *Drifters*, his first film, Grierson quipped, "It will make the viewer seasick!" A visual poem about herring fishing, *Drifters* featured the British workingman on screen for the first time in a heroic role.

3

Father of Documentary Film

When Grierson returned to Britain in 1927, he looked and sounded like a Chicago gangster. With his broad-brimmed fedora, snappy language, and self-confidence, he figured he could turn heads at the Empire Marketing Board (EMB), a new government agency of forty-five departments, none of which was for film. It took a week to get past the entrance, twelve different departmental secretaries, and into the office of EMB head Sir Stephen Tallents, whose gleaming, empty mahogany desktop displayed two phones. The office smelled of fresh paint and the shelves were half-filled with books and neatly stacked files. Behind a deluxe leather chair sat a fatherly public relations official with kind eyes and greying hair who seemed immediately sympathetic. Grierson came on gangbusters. "This place is pretty slow. Seems like it's playing a tune that's Chinese or Dutch, whatever. You know, we have stories right here on the doorstep that are begging to be told and cinema is the pulpit that we should use for propaganda. Here's the pitch: I want to explore and circulate informational films. Traditional education is going nowhere, because it has given people facts, but no faith or imagination."

Tallents liked the unorthodox young man's confident words. "People need drama to excite them to the real world of an Empire that is truly a commonwealth. Just think, a single say-so can be repeated a thousand times a night to a million eyes. If it is good enough, over the years it can reach millions of eyes. This is the new hope – public persuasion." Tallents decided right then to make him his protégé. "Convince the bureaucrats to support your ideas," was all he said, and he turned the Scotsman loose.

For the next two years Grierson exposed functionaries and the British public to exhibits of international educational film. At Victoria Station, London, travellers saw film shorts like Bill Oliver's *Home of the Buffalo*, a breathtaking glimpse of the last North American bison herd shot in western Canada from ground level, while some 45,000 children in Newcastle and Gateshead were introduced to another Canadian scenic, *Rushing Waters*, that hopscotched a dozen waterways across the Dominion, from picturesque streams to the mighty Niagara Falls. Some shows turned heads while others, like *Where the Moose Run*

Loose, left audiences wondering if any people lived in Canada.

There were also screenings of educational films for civil servants and their families. At one show, he featured Russian films. A reactionary Colonel Blimp type rose, and as he stormed out, snorted angrily, "Whoever brought in these films has gone Bolshevik." It was a rare moment as Grierson held his tongue and snickered.

∽

After studying the unpromising financial possibilities for making his own film, Grierson devised a winning gambit: a visually dramatic and naturalist film about the herring industry. "Why herring?" asked Tallents. Grierson had done his homework.

"Because the Minister who holds government purse strings has written a book on herring," he replied. Both Tallents and the Minister took the bait. Grierson was given the go-ahead to become the writer, director, and editor of *Drifters.*

With cameraman Basil Emmott, he planned every shot meticulously. Location shooting at marine laboratories gave him underwater shots of fish. They also filmed bird scenes of gulls and gannets in picturesque locales. When the fishermen failed to land a catch of herring, Grierson bought another ship's catch and tried to fake it. It was not authentic and he scrapped the footage. In documentary, life had to be captured at the source. He ordered the herring drifter out to sea during a gale to capture the authentic pitching of the craft.

While Emmott lay seasick below, Grierson, calling this whole ensemble the "poetics," lashed the camera to the wheelhouse and captured the rogue waves. He even built a set to replicate the ship's interior, and the crew acted as though they were living daily life, from eating to sleeping to joking with the cook. They pretended they were tumbling about as if on the high seas. The effect was perfect. No one ever looked at the camera.

Bringing the story to coherence was what editing was all about. Alone in a London basement room in Belsize Park, he slaved for the next eighteen months. His worldly possessions were a pot, kettle, fry pan, and three dishes. He was still sleeping on a mattress-less cot. One day, Margaret Taylor, a professional editor, arrived to bring order out of the chaos of pieces of film in bins or dangling from a dozen wires stretched wall to wall. "Hungry? I live on eggs. I can cook them for you five dozen ways." They had omelette and drank tea from recycled jam jars as he told her she bore a striking resemblance to his mother. Of course it was love, but it was low-rent. He later boasted mischievously, "Since I could not pay her, I married her." For a year, it was their secret while others were scandalized that they were living in sin. Margaret laughed, both at this and his shabby pants, where a hole in the seat revealed his very slim backside. They were a perfect match for a lifetime.

Drifters opened Sunday afternoon, November 10, 1929 at the prestigious London Film Society. Grierson sat nervously next to Tallents and looked behind at the audience, believing he saw John Maynard Keynes, George Bernard Shaw, and H.G. Wells, all founding members. He thought, *This moment is the culmination of thirty years of life, my service at sea, the years in America, and my conviction that the social use of film will do for people what my family's lighthouse tradition did for ships. It cannot, it must not fail.*

He was right. The sophisticated audience of the British arts elite went wildly enthusiastic. The press raved about how *Drifters* became an instant legend. At a press conference afterwards, Grierson announced, "This is a prototype, a *documentary* film. Its symbolic images link nature, man, and machine. We are happy too that the censors have, after four years, allowed Eisenstein's *Battleship Potemkin* to be shown on the same program."

One critic said, "I notice how its editing technique echoes the Russian's style. Can you comment?"

"Certainly true," Grierson replied. "Especially as you see the men heaving and hauling their nets. But notice too how it uses Robert Flaherty's man-in-nature method. *Drifters'* impressionistic representation of nature is a symbolic expression of the natural forces the fishermen hoped to exploit. There is both a general and abstract truth that links an 'objective' working class with tradition and modernity." Grierson winked as he summarized glibly why the film worked, "Besides, the heaving boat makes people seasick."

A few socialists noted in the left-wing press that unlike Eisenstein's revolutionary workers, Grierson's British working class ignored the battle of labour versus capital. But the socialists were not paying the bill. This was, after all, Britain, where the rule of "no controversy" applied to government activities. Grierson knew that if he was to cultivate more government sponsorship, radical politics were forbidden. "The first rule of filmmaking is don't pistol-whip the hand that holds the wallet," he concluded and added in his best gangster idiom, "You don't give a new swimmer cement shoes."

As they toasted their success at a local pub afterwards, Tallents was surprised to learn that the deliriously happy Grierson did not want to become a filmmaker. "Why not?" he queried. "Because the next film could fail," he answered, swigging his gin. "I want to form a core of ambitious idealists and to make a documentary machine that produces films regularly and successfully. Will you help?"

The wise bureaucrat knew there was no stopping the flamboyant Scotsman. Within a year, some eighteen university-educated men and women were learning their craft. Grierson often called them together for "think sessions" at the pub. There he underscored a basic rule: film was social first and aesthetic second. The trick was to make drama from the ordinary. As the master put it, "You do not point a camera at the world and call it 'documentary.' You tell a story or illuminate a theme by images, much in the way that poetry works. Imagery and movement. And remember, there is no such thing as truth until you have made it into a form. Truth is an interpretation, a perception."

∞

The EMB sent Grierson to Canada's capital early in 1931 to familiarize himself with the Government Motion Picture Bureau, the oldest government film enterprise in the Empire. It was bitter cold in Ottawa as he entered the director's office. "Siddown Mr. Gerston," his host slurred. "Grierson," the unamused visitor corrected. He did not like smelling alcohol on the director's breath at nine in the morning. The inebriated officer continued. "My friends call me 'Colonel,' which is about all I can remember about being in the First World War," he chuckled. "Now you take this operation," he bragged. "The Bureau has equipment that is five years old. Unfortunately we bought it the year sound came to movies, so all our stuff is silent. But we do have a national distribution network that reaches hundreds of locales. The trouble is, that everybody's asleep when we get there and in a deeper sleep when we leave!" He guffawed at his idea of humour. Grierson wondered how this worthless joker ended up in such a powerful position. "Now you take our relationship with the government... Please do. No, seriously though, we have an 'arm's-length' relationship with the Feds. That means they do not dictate to us and we enjoy complete freedom. Trouble is, they give us no money for production, so I spend my budget paying salaries, writing memos, and looking at the latest tourist film showing deer and beaver. It's not that we are forgotten. We just don't exist. Are you sure you won't have a drink?"

Grierson shook his head and smiled. He was angry. He envied the Colonel's freedom from financial and political pressure. After screening the Bureau's tourist films and people-less sunset landscapes, he concluded they were boring. Taking leave of his host, Grierson said adieu and expressed his hope that this was the beginning of a long, fruitful relationship with Canada. (To himself: *And a shorter relationship with the Colonel.*)

∞

Back in Britain, Grierson got lucky: Robert Flaherty agreed to be mentor to the crew working on an industrial craftsmanship documentary. The spendthrift American romantic blew his budget shooting background material on location. After drinks at a Birmingham hotel one evening, Grierson told Flaherty, "Bob, there's good news and bad news. The good news is that every foot of film you have shot has captured the natural forces that make contemporary factory work boring and meaningless. And the shots of craftsmen at work are fascinating. This is going to be a great film."

Amused, Flaherty rocked back on his chair. "I knew it Grierson. So what's bad?"

"Well Bob, your extravagant shooting methods have bankrupted the production. Your number's up."

An uncomprehending and angry Flaherty threatened to resign. Grierson shrugged, "Bob, I accept your resignation. There's no more money."

Flaherty protested, "Go tell the government money guys who I am."

Grierson replied, "That won't work because they think you're a bloody photographer, one of those chaps you see working on holiday beaches." The outraged Flaherty leaped to his full six-feet-plus, knocked over his drink, turned purple, and raised both fists to the heavens. For once he was at a loss for words. Then he hurled invective in rage.

Unmoved, Grierson said, "Sorry, Bob, I hate to let a genius go. You're fired." More swearing. The hotel manager threw them out.

With his young apostles, Grierson edited Flaherty's footage to make *Industrial Britain*, a romantic celebration of disappearing industrial craftsmanship and modern industry. It became the most popular EMB film after *Drifters*.

For four more years, the indomitable Scot supervised production of over one hundred films. He and Margaret remained close to the staff. They welcomed them and other artists to a weekly open house at their new London lodgings, a two-storey Victorian house, where drink and food were plentiful. Margaret's gentle, sympathetic understanding helped smooth over Grierson's slave-driving tendencies. "No sick days!" he bellowed to one complainer. "When I am sick, I have a projector placed in my room so I can continue to critique your work." He told them roughly, "Work early and work late, and if you don't like dog biscuits for pay, then get out." At one soirée featuring the usual ham, blood pudding, and hard-boiled eggs, a young man, made brave by alcohol, tried to pull Grierson off his high horse by accusing him of being a propagandist. Well into his cups, Grierson fired back, as he ran his hand continuously through his sandy hair, his blue eyes blazing. "Of course this is propaganda. Simply put, *propaganda is education*. The 'manipulation' in our films combines aesthetics with ideas of democratic reform. We are medicine men hired to mastermind. We are giving every individual a living conception of the community which he has the privilege to serve... And it is our public duty to serve, dammit!"

The sermons seemed to work and he always had the last word. "Ours is the liberal satisfaction of serving education, of serving the greatest mobilization of the public imagination since the churches lost their grip. Our job is revelation, to inspire faith. Cinema is our pulpit."

These were brave words. Yet his fledgling movement was in trouble. The Great Depression was about to sink his experiment for lack of money. After its production budget was slashed, the EMB received its death notice. Then, miraculously, there appeared a new lease on life. Tallents engineered the entire unit's transfer to Britain's General Post Office in 1933.

Filmmakers were glum to learn their assignment: tell the story of communications. They thought this task would constrict them. "Boys, don't despair," Grierson encouraged. "So long as you can still emphasize the drama of the ordinary on the doorstep, the pattern of contemporary life and the changes going on around us, you can develop the documentary idea and avoid being party to false witness. Bite into the time."

Privately, he feared that the Establishment might squash cinema's real destiny as social commentator and art. Publicly, he put it positively and simply, "Where there's life, there's hope."

4

King of the Showmen

S itting on the back of his chair (for more height) Grierson harangued some filmmakers who had been arguing. "You must see yourselves as part of a movement. I never saw a good film happen unless three or four heads were devoted to it." If having new offices in London's Soho was a serendipitous luxury, he reminded them they had many enemies: "Commercial interests resent a government agency making films. They hate documentary's growing non-theatrical audience. Civil servants call us radicals. We must stay ahead of them all."

Critics insisted that he was his own worst enemy, not just because of his flashy leadership style, combative

In *Housing Problems*, a woman talks about rats in her
tenement. Twenty years later this technique
will be called *cinéma vérité*.

Night Mail was a breathtaking visual and verbal poem
about the postal service. Grierson supervised
both these films.

nature, and unorthodox behaviour, but because he inflated audience statistics. This alienated the Establishment bureaucracy. But as King of the Showmen and public relations specialist/propagandist, Grierson created a documentary mythology, endlessly proselytizing with publications and speeches. His filmmakers adored him because he protected them. As director Harry Watt put it "We were adult enough to laugh at his foibles and play-acting, to joke about his verbosity and Calvinism, but basically, we adored him and could not humiliate him."

Locating new talent was Grierson's great strength. He was fortunate to engage the world-renowned Brazilian-born director, Alberto Cavalcanti, lately from France, to teach the young filmmakers to experiment with sound at the unit's low-budget sound studio at Blackheath, in southeast London. Grierson enjoyed the healthy tension as he argued for social purpose film while pretending to sneer at Cavalcanti's "aestheticky" cinema that tended to tell a story.

There followed a famous exchange with Cavalcanti in the director's chair for the mining classic, *Coal Face* (1935). Cavalcanti was a small man with sensitive, soft, and owlish features, receding wavy brown hair, round dark-framed eyeglasses and alert eyes that took in everything around him. He invited Grierson to see a test print that combined the commentary of a male and female chorus with Benjamin Britten's music, W.H. Auden's verse, and natural sound, all cut rhythmically to match the images.

Grierson swept into the studio theatre, shouted, "Okay, Shoot," to the projectionist, and plunked himself down in the empty first row as he lit a cigarette. He kept crossing and uncrossing his legs and fidgeted noticeably during the test screening. When the lights came up, he tore into Cavalcanti, perhaps unsatisfied by Auden's romantic ode to the "lurcher-loving collier, black as night…" whose Sunday love for a lass is cut short by Monday, "…When none may kiss, be marble to his soot, and to his black be white." Frustrated, Cavalcanti listened to Grierson blasting aesthetics for the umpteenth time. The assembled half-dozen film-makers' frightened smiles were chiselled on their faces. "This is turning out to be a too arty experiment," Grierson criticized. "Remember, the word 'documentary' impresses the government as something serious."

In an uncharacteristic display of emotional nastiness, Cavalcanti fired back, "Yes as something dusty and something annoying…"

"Now Cav, you are really a very innocent character," growled Grierson, trying another tack. He thought of his mother's soup kitchen for unemployed miners. "If you ease up on the experimental aesthetics, you might find that aesthetic quality lies in the mere lucidity of exposition. Get down to the philosophical message of this film, the issue of exploited mine workers. Direct description, simple analysis and a commanding conclusion. Show light where there was darkness. Being 'aestheticky' means that you're in it for your own blue eyes. Enough aesthetics, dammit!"

Cavalcanti's struggle to give creative shape to the complex film left the normally gentle artist on a short fuse. He shot back, "You know Grierson, my English may be rotten, but I do know this. The opposite of aesthetic is ANAESTHETIC and I won't do that!" Grierson coloured deep red before the assembled group, stomped on his cigarette, wheeled around and stormed out, muttering expletives. He did not speak to Cavalcanti for a week.

But he let Cavalcanti prevail because the artist's technical knowledge and facility with sound were colossal. After *Coal Face*'s qualified success, Grierson tricked Auden and Britten into collaboration again in 1936. He told each that the other had accepted his invitation to work on the next project – a typical Grierson ploy. That film, *Night Mail*, became the defining classic of the GPO Film Unit. Its images of wires and rails and men and speed gave drama to the story of the postal train from London to Glasgow as it screamed through the night to its morning destination.

Using accelerated montage, here was a visual cornucopia: shots of racing engine wheels, cross-cut with rabbits scurrying in panic as the train roared over hill and dale; match cuts of telegraph lines with rails; and railway ties that flew by in a blur. When it was done, Grierson said directors Basil Wright and Harry Watt had delivered "a kick in the belly" to an enthusiastic public. Cavalcanti supervised cutting Auden's verse to fit the visuals, Britten's music to link it to the beat of the train's wheels, and a narration that at one point was read at top speed to sound like the clickety-clack of rail cars:

> Letters of thanks, letters from banks,
> Letters of joy for the girls and boys,
> Receipts and bills and invitations...
> With applications for situations

And timid lovers' declarations;
And gossip, gossip from all the nations
News substantial, news financial...
Grierson himself read the last lines:
And none will hear the postman's knock
Without a quickening of the heart,
For who can bear to feel himself forgotten?

This simple story of mail delivery turned into a human melodrama with a strong narrative line about loneliness and companionship. Shown theatrically and non-theatrically, *Night Mail* reached several million Britons.

∞

Grierson's sister, Ruby, was among the early "graduates" of the movement. She had the same forthright devil-may-care manner as her brother, and was equally direct. One evening, as they were having dinner with Margaret, Ruby turned and said critically, "John, you see everything like a goldfish in a bowl. I want to break the bowl."

He was not very surprised at the Grierson belligerence, and decided to play along. "And what, my dear little sister, do you propose to do?"

She pushed her plate away and stared. Their eyes met, identical beams of blue phosphorous, searing into each other. They could have melted steel. "John, the movement's films are detached and impersonal, full of industrial and commercial spectacle, but lacking social truth."

He was used to hearing this complaint and of making the same reply, "The government pays the bills.

I practise the art of the possible – we go so far and then have to stop. You know how they can hamstring us."

"Precisely," she continued. "That is why Arthur Elton, Edgar Anstey, and I have approached the gas company. They will let us film South London slum dwellers. I'll direct a journalistic spotlight that shows the poverty of Depression-wracked Britain honestly. The gas utility wants people to associate them with public well-being, and we know just how to do it."

Her brother swallowed the last of his shepherd's pie, slugged back his gin, and re-lit his ever-present cigarette. He surprised Ruby. "Congratulations little sister. It's about time we increased the breadth and scope of the documentary. You have my unconditional blessing."

The team set up equipment on location in a Stepney, south London one-room slum tenement. The wallpaper, a nondescript, barely visible flower pattern, was grey with age and had peeled off from the ceiling halfway to the floor where leaky water had coloured everything brown. A large hole in the ceiling looked as though a missile had been shot through it. A pitcher and basin on a rickety table substituted for running water. A hole in a plank was the indoor toilet. A single beat-up chair seemed to hold up the sagging wall.

The crew used a Mitchell camera, which allowed ten minutes of shooting nonstop, and which weighed as much as three men. They lit the hovel with two 500-watt lamps powered by seven 12-volt car batteries in a vehicle parked outside. Ruby, like her brother, used her knack for stimulating casual conversation. The round, clean-faced Cockney woman of the house, Mrs. Atride, her neatly combed black hair pinned back, stood grasping the chipped metal frame of the bed to tell her story. Dressed in a plain white dress that could have passed for a hospital gown covering her tubelike body, she wore her best necklace, a string of black beads.

Ignoring the camera in the doorway, the lights shining through the window, and the sound truck with its huge sound equipment, the feisty matron described the battle to kill a ferocious rat. Her reed-thin husband stood next to her, wearing his cloth worker's cap. His Sunday vest covered a wrinkled shirt with sleeves rolled to the elbows. He nodded silently in agreement as if to punctuate the truth of her story. The visuals, coupled with authentic sound, marked the birth of what is called today *cinéma vérité* (direct cinema).

Mrs. Atride began, "We pay ten shillings a week for this room where I don't have room to swing a cat around. One night I says, 'Mike, there's our Old Gentleman inside the 'ouse again' and he says, 'Nonsense, you're crackers.' Well, he jumped down to find 'im under the bed and he throws 'is clothes on 'im, but he got away. Mike grabbed a broom and knocked 'im down on the ground. Then he come up, but Mike had the jump on 'im and beat 'im to death with the broom. Of course his screams was terrible…"

Housing Problems' social realism demonstrated an alternative to the formal and impersonal documentaries of the GPO and served as a beacon to future documentarians who wanted the camera to capture life as it unfolded. Ruby and John were thrilled at its success.

A nervous British government kept hearing rumours that documentary equalled communist subversion, so it planted a mole in the operation as an editor-in-training. The filmmakers made his life hell. One day a couple of them huddled just close enough to barely be heard. "All right for tonight, Joe? Got the bomb? The job's on." The terrified agent did not know whether to blow the whistle or to admit his cover was blown. He transferred out. Everyone, including Grierson, had a good laugh.

When he was attacked for his "leftwing atheistic politics," Grierson lashed out in self-defence, "I've been brought up as a Calvinist. The more I've lived, the more I think that the Christian religion was a savage attack on the human race by the Jews. When I think of religion I believe in Spinoza's God... As to religion itself, like the obscure French duchess wrote, *'Religion, c'est comme le sexe. Je le fais souvent, mais je n'en parle jamais.'"* [Religion is like sex. I do it often but I never talk about it.]

By 1937, the British government was sorry it had started the documentary movement and prepared to wind it down. Grierson left the GPO for Film Centre, a hub in Soho, London, where he advised and co-ordinated key creative personnel. Friday night screenings there became well known, and prominent figures from the arts world like Laszlo Moholy-Nagy and Paul Hindemith, both in London after fleeing Nazi Germany, would drop in to see the latest work, drink, and talk. His coffee cup half-full of gin and a cigarette omnipresent in his right hand, Grierson loved after hours in the company of visitors like D.W. Griffith, Josef Von Sternberg, and Robert Flaherty. These soirées helped keep the young artists together. "We were living the English equivalent of café life in Paris," remarked one.

Film Centre produced a host of documentaries on food, schools, health, and air pollution for some major British companies that wanted to embellish their public image. Some critics on the left complained that the films did not go far enough in their analysis of contemporary Britain. Others on the right were sure that the filmmakers were all communists. Some insiders thought it remarkable that the movement found sponsorship at all.

Grierson faced the criticism with the bravado that made him a legend. As they raised their glasses at the Highlander Pub, he said, "Now boys," (the young men vastly outnumbered the women) "you know we are serving the greatest mobilization of the public imagination since the churches lost their grip. And I would sooner have an educational system based on the Church and on Christian virtues than a national educational system that prefers knowledge to faith."

The faith, he continued, was not the synthetic lie of partisan politics, nor was it radical solutions. "We shoot on location and feature real people. We are shining a spotlight on mass man's place in the world."

"What about our political adversaries?" a shy new talent asked. Grierson's familiar rejoinder for the last eight years surprised none of the veterans. "My view is that we are entering upon a new society, which is neither capitalist nor socialist but one in which we can achieve central planning without losing individual initiative... We have to grasp the historical process and not bother about recriminations or moral strictures. Art should be used as a hammer, not a mirror."

But Grierson had gone as far as he could go in Britain – perhaps too far. When Canada requested his expertise to survey the dominion government's film activities, he accepted. Besides, he was stung by the British Council's refusal to screen the documentary movement's best films at the 1939 New York World's Fair; the Council charged that the films were too radical. Grierson packed his bags. He believed serendipity was about to change his life and career once again. And like others, he wondered if disintegrating political events in Europe meant another world war was imminent.

Stuart Legg (left) and John Grierson (right) at the wartime
National Film Board. Grierson wanted to point Canada to the
future. "The message? National unity and understanding. The
documentary film should become the searchlight of democracy."

5

A Secret Agent?

O ne late night in the spring of 1936, just as Grierson
and Alberto Cavalcanti were sparring over the best
way to lay the sound track for *Night Mail*, there arrived at
the London sound studio a short, amiable Canadian, Ross
McLean. His letter of introduction announced he was
secretary to Canada's High Commissioner to London,
Vincent Massey. The busy, irascible Grierson, now in the
fourteenth hour of his day, was about to dismiss the
intruder when he recalled that in a trip to Canada in 1931,
he had written a report recommending that the Canadian
Government Motion Picture Bureau be restructured to
include more films with people and fewer with wildlife
and trees. He did not even read McLean's letter.

"What does Massey want?" he snarled. The academically inclined, ever gentle McLean replied, "I have been a lifetime film buff and was a co-founder of Canada's National Film Society. His Excellency wants me to observe what the British documentarians are up to."

"Sit down and keep quiet," replied Grierson, and obediently, the demure Canadian pulled out a notepad and disappeared into a corner.

Massey had told McLean to recommend what might be done to improve the quality of Canadian government films. For the next four hours he sat in awe as the remarkable *Night Mail* was born. After watching the creative team, McLean believed this dynamic Scotsman could mix a tonic for Canada to help improve its tourist films as well as the image of its unphotogenic prime minister, William Lyon Mackenzie King.

Back at the Canadian Legation, McLean enthused, "That film is a real kick in the belly. Grierson is so far ahead of the Canadians, he might help us increase the quality and quantity of our films. He told me we were wasting our money making forgettable films on industry and natural resources. As for film subjects, he calls Canada 'Oklahoma territory, waiting to be opened, the frontier of the future.' He says he could put the Bureau back into business as leader of the pack."

A year passed before Ottawa invited Grierson to Canada in June 1938 to survey government film activity. He crossed the Dominion, meeting politicians, newspapermen and other prominent Canadian educators. His report lambasted the tired and dispirited

Motion Picture Bureau. "Most of the films seem to be about parks and holidays, and the majority of the material that finds its way into American newsreels is useless," he said with his usual bluntness. "The Bureau could regain its position as a world leader by developing the newsreel to make Canada better known internationally," he continued. "Canada should forget pretending to be a big, innocent, baby-hearted, holiday haunt... It needs more films about real people. Once in a while somebody must do some work that might be connected to the real Canada," he groused. "The weakness of Canada? It is a country still asleep. The Motion Picture Bureau lacks direction, is weak and is unable to carry out a dynamic film policy, and the government departments are selfish and petty."

Grierson's pen became the light that awoke the sleeping capital. Important people were impressed. He recommended that Ottawa create a central agency under a film officer to advise and co-ordinate all government film work and film distribution. In January 1939 the government approved the plan to create a new centralizing agency, to be called the National Film Board of Canada (NFB). It was to have eight members. "This board is not being established with the intention of providing jobs for anybody," Grierson promised. "The Film Board is to be largely administrative. There is really to be only one paid man in the organization." The chief executive officer was to be the government film commissioner and the Motion Picture Bureau was to continue producing government films except if the film commissioner decided they should be done by commercial firms or by a government department itself. An uninterested Parliament passed the bill creating the National Film Board and it received royal assent on May 2, 1939.

By the fall, the film commissioner's job was still vacant, because no Canadian had enough experience to qualify. Six years later, there stood a well-lubricated film propaganda machine of nearly eight hundred employees and a forgotten pledge of "no jobs for anybody." Standing astride the colossus was John Grierson, with amiable Ross McLean as his assistant. Grierson and the documentary were to become synonymous with Canadian film.

∞

In 1939 Britain still hoped for peace, but prepared for war. Few in Ottawa knew that Grierson was fulfilling another critical assignment for the British: to set up a North American propaganda base to urge Canada, and more importantly, the United States, into a partnership with London if war broke out. He was to do the same for Australia and New Zealand. Decades later, in his best James Bond imitation, Grierson would boast, "Yes, I was a secret agent for the British Government during the Second World War."

Because he was a man who never stopped talking, Grierson was a terrible "secret" agent. When war exploded in September, he sent an uninspired message to London, "American opinion is not with Britain and isolationism is still strong," he wrote. In dopey reply, the British scolded him for sending telegrams from the British embassy without using code. Grierson wished he could be more useful, but it was hard for the American public to take the war seriously as newsreels showed upper class Britons wearing decorative gas masks. It took President Roosevelt to steer public opinion as he defended his government's decision to "loan" ships and materiel to Britain as one would loan a garden hose to a neighbour whose house was on fire. Even though this "phoney war" continued until spring, 1940, his message convinced many Americans to prepare for the worst.

Meanwhile, back in drowsy Ottawa, there was no one qualified to run the still headless National Film Board. Having failed as a secret agent, Grierson agreed to accept the job for six months until they could find a Canadian. Agreeing to "help out," he remained in charge for the next six years.

His was a scattered operation which by 1941 occupied five different locations in the capital, the main one being a former lumber mill perched on the banks of the Ottawa River. Grierson described it as a "largish ugly building opposite the embassy of Vichy France... a busy joint housing the whole Canadian production set-up." The old mill had a permanent smell of sawdust and was used round the clock, with teams working in shifts. It was also a firetrap. Had the Ottawa fire department not been so close by, the whole operation could have gone up in smoke when there were little accidents on several occasions.

The new commissioner insisted on one operating principle: there has to be maximum interchange of information between everyone and maximum individual responsibility for everyone. Staff learned their film-making skills from the bottom up.

From forty films in production, distribution, or preparation the first year, by 1943 there were two hundred, all being used in one way or another as "a supplementary system of national education," according to Grierson. "This National Film Board plan is a service to the Canadian public and a light to other nations," he boasted to a friend in Britain. In his usual exaggerated style, he insisted the NFB was a way to mobilize the nation's imagination and energy as they created Canada's future. "My goal is to carry the message of unity and understanding to every Canadian and to people abroad. We intend to shape the documentary film as a searchlight of democracy."

There was one difficult customer to please, Prime Minister Mackenzie King. The camera-shy and radio-allergic leader of Canada admitted reluctantly to aides that information had to become a priority in the war. No wonder. Physically he was short, overweight, and had a high-pitched unattractive voice that never sounded natural. King listened in despair to Winston Churchill's inspiring speeches. He could never match that confident voice with his own words quivering off key. King detested his own voice so much that by the time he finished revising his speeches for radio, the rhetoric was gone and he was left with lifeless words. As a typical modest English Canadian, he hated the spotlight on himself almost as much as he hated propaganda.

Grierson understood this and tried to create a more commanding prime ministerial image. In one newsreel, King sat behind his desk addressing two underlings with their backs to the audience. The prime minister was trying to show leadership by explaining

Canada's war aims. Time and again he flubbed his lines, whether in close-up, medium shot, or long shot. Sweating profusely after a dozen takes, he wiped his brow and finally squeezed the words out, but they sounded hollow. The film crew shook their heads in disbelief as they left the Prime Minister's Office. That evening, King, still uncomfortable with the very word *propaganda* as well as personal publicity, confided to his diary, "I loathe my own appearance on the screen."

The prime minister needed a shot of adrenaline. He had told aides he had sworn off drinking alcohol (at least until the war was over). To himself, he promised to stop attending séances where he had talked to his dead mother and dead dog Pat through mediums. His one indulgence was keeping a daily diary into which he poured his most intimate thoughts about politics, politicians and things mystical. "I see the hands of the clock are now just on eleven and twelve," he wrote secretively. "This is very significant." Only he understood why this was so.

Given his lack of charisma and nervousness in public, one must ask how King managed to stay Canada's longest serving prime minister. The answer was that the lonely bachelor spent most of his time observing what all the other politicians were doing. In a small city like Ottawa, he monitored everything going on in his party and then spent his spare time recording his opinions in his secret diary. From noting how afraid he was of flying (the plane might crash) to treating his government's expenditures as though they were from his own household budget ("Grierson may not set up an overseas film unit because it would cost an unnecessary

$125,000"), King supervised everything. It took until 1941 to form that unit, the Canadian Army Film Unit (CAFU), which the Americans trained for free.

King was no personality, but he wanted an information bureau to serve as a counterweight to Canada's powerful press. He told the new Bureau of Public Information, "Neither mislead the public nor advertise the government but make the Canadian war effort better known." Giving the nod to Grierson, King told the Bureau to finance the National Film Board's wartime newsreel for cinemas, *Canada Carries On*. It was an instant hit, with a new twenty-minute item for cinemas each month.

King did not like Grierson much, even though the NFB chief cultivated a number of allies close to the prime minister. In January, 1940 the Scotsman blundered into the first of a series of fatal mistakes that would ruin his career. Ottawa was in a deep freeze, and Grierson was at the plush, red-carpeted Rideau Club, sitting in one of its deep and comfortable chesterfields, drinking with the top man from the Canadian Motion Picture Distributors Association, plying him with charm and alcohol to get a better deal for Film Board distribution in commercial theatres. As he spoke, Grierson could only think how nice it would be to finish his British assignment, co-ordinating the distribution of documentary films in Australia and New Zealand, where at present it was summer. Naively, he thought things would go smoother if he left this man in charge of the Film Board while he was gone for a few months. He neglected to ask about this gentleman's politics. He learned later that the man he had left in charge of the NFB was best friends with King's arch foe, Premier Hepburn of Ontario.

Grierson had arranged that an American newsreel be shot in Canada, *The March of Time: Canada at War.* The newsreel made favourable reference to King on the eve of the 1940 federal election. Premier Hepburn leaned on Grierson's replacement to delay its release, which he did. A King adviser went to see the acting commissioner in Grierson's spartan office in the old lumber mill. Sitting down next to stacks of canned film reels, he said, "Two can play this game. I hear the Customs Office might hold up the importation of Paramount films into Canada." Friend of Premier Hepburn or not, this was Famous Players' bread and butter. And Famous Players was *his* bread and butter. The acting NFB chief released the film.

But Hepburn had other friends. Soon the Ontario Board of Censors banned the film's provincial release. King seethed in anger. "Where's Grierson?" he snapped bitterly, unaware that his film commissioner was in summertime and in another hemisphere. When he was told that Grierson was both absent and responsible for this blundering choice of replacement, his mind was set: the Scotsman was reckless, too much concerned for his own little kingdom, and less worried for King. The prime minister's advisers reacted quickly and cleverly. They advertised in Ottawa newspapers for people to cross the river to Quebec and "see the film banned in Ontario." King won the election by a landslide in March. He summed up his feelings about the episode to one confidante, "Grierson is an outsider who does not understand Canadian politics."

But King needed a cosmetic makeover. He invited the suntanned Grierson to dinner. On the personal level, as usual, the flamboyant Scotsman used overkill to sell himself. Mindful of the prime minister's opposition to both the word and the usually accepted meaning of propaganda, Grierson blew into Laurier House like a spring windstorm.

He climbed the five stairs at the entrance, and noticed its wooden entry was painted black. *Curious*, he thought. *This doorway contrasts dramatically with the house's friendly yellow brick*, and thinking of Number 10 Downing Street, he noted the Canadian prime ministerial residence was so humble as to be ordinary. A servant took his coat and he entered the main drawing room. It was not bigger than a typical late nineteenth-century living room. A white brick fireplace, surrounded by a hand-carved dark chestnut mantle and façade, threw off considerable heat. The wall above it was divided into three panels in a light-coloured wood, each framed by a mahogany arch. Two adjoining walls were filled with bookshelves and four sets of same-colour leather bindings. The mantel, framed by brass lamps on the wall, was cluttered with nondescript knick-knacks; a small picture of a terrier (King's dead dog Pat) was placed left of its centre, where there stood a traditional mantel clock in a solid walnut case that sounded Westminster chimes every quarter hour. Grierson thought it must be a clock similar to thousands of others in Canadian middle-class homes. A second, smaller clock stood at the far end. King was consumed by Time.

The prime minister reminded Grierson of a plump chicken, his pink facial skin sagging somewhat, his pince-nez balanced on the end of his nose. He was dressed as always, in formal attire, a grey man in a grey suit and tie. A handkerchief in his vest pocket was crumpled, a sign that he used it often. He sat in a dark comfortable armchair, an open book on his lap, and an English porcelain cup of tea on a mahogany side table. "Come right in Mr. Grierson," he spoke in his high-pitched voice and he gestured to an empty matching chesterfield for his guest to sit down. "I have sworn off alcohol for the duration of the war, but you are welcome to indulge. Ley? Bring Mr. Grierson an aperitif."

"Gin. Thank you, Prime Minister. Weather in Ottawa is the only thing I cannot yet abide. My doorman tells me that when he exceeds half a bottle a day, either an inch of rain has fallen or the thermometer is below zero." King tried to smile unsuccessfully.

As Grierson accustomed himself to the ambience and the smell of dankness and age in the air, he noticed a light shining in the corner. It illuminated a large gold-framed painting of a white-haired woman in quarter profile before a fireplace, some crocheting on her lap. King could not help but notice Grierson admiring the prominent work of art.

"That is my dear departed mother. She is still my guide as we march through parlous times. Do you think, Mr. Grierson, it is possible to commune with those who have been closest to us but are now departed?"

Grierson did not take the bait. " I cannot say, but I do know this, Prime Minister. In the heart of every Scotsman the musical verses of Robbie Burns and the clatter of the Battle of Bannockburn speak as though they are still present. And the reason? Education. It is only through learning that the past remains alive and the present can be articulated with verve. And film is what I know best. Here is a medium that can bring Canada alive to itself, can express the excellences of Canada, can secure the future of Canada and..."

"Yes, quite," the prime minister interrupted. "But you see, Mr. Grierson, there is more to the living than the here and now. There are areas of the brain that we hardly yet understand."

"Right, sir," Grierson enjoined, completely missing King's thrust. "That is why on seeing your mother's portrait, I thought about how she must have had the Scots temperament to see that her son's education, (Harvard, wasn't it?) was the very best, and that her son would finish the job one hundred years later that her father, your grandfather, William Lyon Mackenzie, began in 1837." King, not impressed, took out his handkerchief and wiped his brow. He sensed Grierson was trying too hard.

During dinner, Grierson, lubricated by additional alcohol, explained soothingly to King how propaganda was nothing to fear: "We will not use propaganda to exploit, but to inform and to develop national unity. I intend to give visual meaning to your call for a spirit of mutual tolerance and respect for fundamental human rights – I agree, these are the foundation of Canadian national unity." He continued delivering his favourite speech and repeated that propaganda was, first and last, education. He noticed the prime minister seemed distracted, and again was wiping his brow. Perhaps he was overheated from the fireplace, or perhaps he was thinking about his recent awful Film Board performance.

To win him back, Grierson returned to the virtues of the Scottish tradition that they both shared: a respect for education. "With education, we can bring the United States into the war by concentrating simply on information, cultural relations, and the democratic issues at stake."

Grierson tried more banter with the reluctant King. He noted that both came from Scots antecedents and they both had blue eyes. King spent the evening somberly, wiping his brow frequently while the garrulous Grierson went on about lighthouses, his ancestors, and famous Scots battles. Afterward, King remained underwhelmed. He confided to his diary a brief sentence to summarize the entire evening, "I was much impressed with Grierson's knowledge of the whole work of propaganda, publicity, etc. but not particularly taken with his personality. Still, he is the best man available to carry out a really effective programme for films of the war effort. I have asserted my authority and we shall have a review of the various public agencies involved with public information." Soon he streamlined things by folding the old Government Motion Picture Bureau into the Film Board.

He left Grierson to run the whole enterprise. Grierson, unaware of King's true feelings for him, now thought he enjoyed a special relationship with the prime minister and used the imaginary relationship for all it was worth. Privately, the prime minister told his aides that if Grierson wanted an appointment, he was unavailable. He told them that they should handle any problems.

As film commissioner, Grierson confided to his trusty assistant McLean that he had twisted the arm of the film industry to distribute NFB films in Canada's commercial theatres. Famous Players Canada (owned by Paramount of Hollywood) paid fees to the Film Board to show the *Canada Carries On* newsreel series in its eight hundred theatres every month. "How did you manage that?" asked an incredulous McLean.

The wily Grierson explained, "The film industry is all Jewish, and this bloody war, which I understand is very much Hitler's war against the Jews, gives the Jewish movie executives no second thoughts about distributing and paying for government propaganda." His eyes twinkled mischievously as he continued, "Also, last month, I waved my drink at a cocktail party as if I had one too many, and confided to a friend loudly enough to be heard by two visiting Hollywood types, 'If Canadian theatres refuse to screen government produced shorts, I'll use my direct line to the prime minister and force the issue.'" Bravado was all in a day's work for the clever Scotsman, but when King heard this story, he chafed. Grierson enjoyed no such direct line.

On his first day at the agency, a young writer sat in the only free chair in Grierson's office. The clutter was severe, with film cans piled high on a corner table, and stacks of manila folders spilling out paper of all different colours on another. He squirmed uncomfortably as

the boss, feet hoisted on his desk, kept being interrupted by a ringing phone into which he barked curt
orders. All the while Grierson's steely blue eyes pene-
trated him as he spoke to one person after another on
the other end of the line. Finally he hung up and
addressed the young writer, his finger pointing at him
like an arrow.

"Just understand what we are endeavouring to
do," he explained. "You have to see the perspectives,
the growing points behind what's going on up here on
the Hill. A nation at war; but still bemused. Still half
asleep. You have to search, to analyse, to articulate the
potential of Canada and make it so compelling that
people will want to plunge their hands into their own
pockets. Their own pockets. You understand?"

Grierson jabbed a hole in the air as he spoke, ran
his finger round quickly inside his collar, jerked his
head impatiently, scratched his scalp, lowered his feet
from his desk, then hoisted them up again. He was
bent and poised like a coiled spring. He seemed wound
up tighter than a watch, yet perfectly in control.

He pushed his chair back, leaped up, and paced
the room like Groucho Marx, talking nonstop. He
crushed out a cigarette and lit another. "Dammit, the
Yanks are clueless, enjoying their pie and ice cream
while in Canada, people are searching for leadership,
looking for matches to light the dark. Make images that
will straighten their shoulders, brighten their eyes, put
spine into them," he urged. "Give them the images
they know: hockey rinks, maple syrup, mountains,
prairie combines," he continued. "Write a script to
time for nine minutes and put the visuals in the right

margin to guide the director. All right, you got that? Now get the hell out of my office."

The young writer left the office convinced he could do anything, anything the boss wanted. Something dynamic had touched him – a human whirlwind.

Behind the swaggering, Grierson was trying to transplant to Canada a documentary style that revealed the underlying essence of the times rather than the superficial details of daily life. As he explained, "A person's private concerns are not for documentary. Aesthetics must have equal status with social purposiveness." He told the young Canadians, "Your job is to reveal the historical forces that are the bedrock of society. They include ethical values such as strength, simplicity, energy, directness, hardness, decency, courage, and duty." He defined these as "masculine." He continued, "I am not at all interested in 'negative' ethical values such as sophistication, sentimentality, excessive sexuality, homosexuality, bohemianism, nostalgia, status seeking and social climbing. I define these as 'feminine.'" Grierson might claim to be a progressive, but when it came to feminist ideas, he was a product of his age.

∽

It was January 1941, a typical winter's day in Ottawa – dark at 4 p.m. and minus 20 degrees Celsius. Snow was falling like a white curtain as Grierson invited a few of his brightest filmmakers out for a drink at the Chateau Laurier, whose hotel bar was a favourite locale for

Ottawa's political and civil service elite. As they entered the large room, the first impression was the smell of leather chairs and wood polish. One of them stumbled, tripped by the deep pile of the brown and maroon wool carpets. Several stylish Art Deco light fixtures spaced equidistant on the ceiling, had large half-moon shaped milk glass bowls suspended in brass rings that threw off a soft yellow light. Perhaps two dozen professional looking people were talking quietly at different tables. Drawing three tables together, Grierson said he wanted to discuss the documentary idea, which, unbeknownst to them, he was putting into a manuscript he would publish in 1946 as *Grierson on Documentary*.

After two hours they had consumed enough alcohol to loosen their tongues considerably. The young artists were on the verge of drunkenness, but Grierson had stayed focused. Alcohol did not make him inarticulate, even if it was slowly destroying his body. "Do you know what is at the core of the documentary idea?" he asked, pointing his finger at a neophyte female director.

"Certainly," answered the young woman. "We need to show Canadians and the world that Hitler and the Japanese can be beaten by the combined superior military might of the Allies."

"I thought bending minds by showing reality was our business," ventured another uncertainly.

"Both wrong," Grierson replied, lighting another cigarette. "Who gives a damn about the shot and shell of war? We need to prepare for the peace, to convince audiences that peace can be more exciting than war."

"Maybe," offered an editor, "but I have been working on some extraordinary footage of British

Spitfires shooting down German bombers. *That* is going to make audiences feel good."

"Do you know what Immanuel Kant gave to the world?" Grierson shot back as he gulped his drink. "It was philosophical idealism. He said that aesthetics are as important as taking in what is real – Why? Because it is only through intuition and aesthetic experience that we can understand what is really real. *Feeling* the real world that is abstract and general is just as important as *seeing* the things we can easily comprehend."

"Look," he continued. "You show the Spitfire blasting the Nazi sons of Satan out of the sky and you and the audience think you have seen something. But the viewer has to feel something more... that behind the dogfight is a people's army that has an inner strength, a stubborn calm which iron and steel and bombs can never pierce. That is of greater significance than fire in the sky. Have you put that in your film? You should be using documentary naturalism with dramatic editing techniques – that is how documentary is the creative treatment of actuality."

The group sat in stunned silence. He had just given them the key to a film that up to then had been a series of dogfights with no heart. The film became *Churchill's Island*. In 1942 it won the first ever Academy Award for best documentary short. That was how the Grierson magic worked. He rose, glanced at his watch and said, "My eighteen-hour workday is only half over. The prime minister has asked me to fix the government's information setup. You all owe me another two hours. Get back to work." He threw on his coat and hat and whooshed out the door.

6

Canada's Propaganda Maestro

It was still snowing as Grierson trudged from the Chateau Laurier bar back to the West Block on Parliament Hill. Wrapping his coat collar around his exposed neck, he pulled down his black bowler hat, painted white with snow, to cover half his ears. He entered the threshold through which the high and mighty of Canada passed, and coughed hoarsely into his ungloved hand as a Mounted Policeman checked his identification. *I must remember to dress more warmly,* he thought, *to not keep forgetting my gloves, and to stop smoking so much.* At the end of the corridor, he entered the dark oak door whose letters read Prime Minister's Office. He sat down on the government-issue hardwood

A huge crowd in Ottawa enjoys the NFB Academy Award winner, *Churchill's Island*. In a pre-television age, outdoor public screenings and other non-theatrical venues helped Canadians become aware of war aims and issues.

office chair. He felt himself sliding forward involuntarily. *These chairs are so functional, he mused, But bloody uncomfortable, probably to keep civil servants from falling asleep. They will probably last till 2005 and beyond.*"

The prime minister's assistant, Walter Turnbull, met him. Here was the perfect gatekeeper, tall and dark haired, with intelligent hawk eyes that seemed to peer through the person being addressed, looking for any sign of ill intention. No, he could not see King just now. He was out, but the P.M. was complaining. "He says our national information policy is unfocused and under regular attack in Parliament for being unimaginative, uninspiring, and late. His enemies in the House complain that our overall national effort is earnest, but limited. And the newspapers won't use our facts and statistics. How can you fix it?"

Grierson was piqued that he could not talk to King directly. Either the prime minister did not want to see him, was angry with him, or was indeed too busy. But the Scotsman's sense of public duty was stronger than his ego. "All right then," he began. "the problem is the conservative corporate public relations executives, advertisers, and promotion men who run the information setup. The whole propaganda machine needs vitamin D, and the Americans, whose typical newspaper mentions Canada once in forty-five days, need to be reached through daily news and newsreels."

Turnbull, the ever-protective prime ministerial aide, had a habit of never saying more than was necessary. He always saw the big political picture and went right to the point. "Mr. King fears the country might fracture along English/French lines as it did in World War I. He wants you to be General Manager of the Wartime Information Board for a year while continuing your leadership at the NFB. Can you handle it?"

Grierson coughed again and rasped, "Give me a free hand and I'll show you how to run the social adult education business for keeps."

∞

At the Wartime Information Board (WIB), just as at the NFB, Grierson was a wizard, and soon he became the most talked-about personality in Ottawa. The press referred to him as "Canada's Propaganda Maestro." He hired social scientists to take over where the advertising men had failed. Their assignment: Develop an integrated education in practical citizenship.

He wrote to an old friend in England that Canadians needed to get in touch with essentials and to reverse what he called "the unconsciously fascist process" then operating. "Canadians suffer from a national incapacity for conscious self-measurement and a fantastic sense of want," he wrote perceptively. "We are certainly not going to try to dope people into a false estimate of things that are badly, or unimaginatively, or unprogressively done," he claimed.

"I picture a kind of ministry of Education, where the words 'information,' 'education,' and 'propaganda' are interchangeable. As for the war itself," he admitted frankly, "I can't ever get very excited about the war effort per se; ...the surface values... guns... campaigns and braveries and assembly lines and sacrifices are, taken by themselves, the greatest bore on earth."

His recipe? It was a typical Griersonian aphorism: "A new activism in education and education in action." People had to be made aware of the new citizenship of the co-operative state. "Expand information services to include industrial morale, consumer education, agricultural production, conservation, and nutrition," he urged.

Three months later, he was back in Turnbull's office sitting on the slippery hardwood chair. Again, the prime minister was not available. Grierson's choice of words shocked the staid Turnbull. "What we have been doing has been being totalitarian for the good. Our idea is to be democratic in a practical way, building a hub of media people (like newspaper editors) to develop democratic themes. They'll become a national moral conscience and will take their cue from Ottawa," he explained.

Turnbull told King of the plan. Reluctantly, the prime minister approved Grierson's propaganda line: this was a people's war for social security and human welfare. He allowed Grierson to engage polling firms for the first time to listen to the public. The Cabinet War Committee was afraid to publish the results. They ordered him to stop. Grierson argued that polls, now used by the U.S. and the U.K., were essentially democratic. King brokered a compromise. "There will be a monthly survey to test public opinion and morale," he announced. "We may use it to argue a point or policy. But the survey must remain confidential."

Grierson had won half a loaf, but government insiders still viewed polls suspiciously. To them, information involved a one-way process from the leaders to the led. They resented him when he proved Parliament wrong: Polls showed that the public was not *against* wartime price and wage controls. Some politicians never forgave him for raining on their parade. They had insisted the public *did* oppose them.

"Watch out for St. John and his disciples!" laughed another aide to the prime minister. As propaganda maestro, Grierson loved the spotlight. He was everywhere, making speeches, writing newspaper columns, and preaching his Gospel. In one article, he called for rallying the democratic masses and getting them to forget precious individualism. The educated classes needed to convince the masses there was a greater good – the State itself and victory over Fascism.

The prime minister, liberal to the core, never really warmed up to government information, other than as needed during the national emergency. When the tide turned in July 1943, and it became clear that the Nazis would never win, King planned to close down the information machine when war ended.

Grierson's hectic physical pace drove him to exhaustion in 1943. "My doctor says I am now walking like a ninety-year-old, but he doesn't spend as much time as I do negotiating this rotten winter weather. They say this is the coldest winter in forty years. Good thing Canadians don't wear kilts." His cough worsened and at last he collapsed. His doctor told him to take some months' break or be prepared to crash and burn with a major heart attack. He and Margaret left for Florida, where, instead of soaking up the southern sun, he set to work on another manuscript that would be called *The Eyes of Democracy*. A political Show and Tell, and dangerous to his masters, it would not be published until 1990.

Florida was the perfect tonic. Margaret loved the warmth, which helped relieve the pain in her lifelong crippled hip, and she enjoyed their long conversations, which helped her husband develop his media theory.

They sat on cushioned rattan chairs on the veranda of an old Sarasota guesthouse. The daily rain had stopped and the warm air was heavy, but not oppressive with dampness. He, notepad on his lap, sipped a mint julep, while Margaret enjoyed iced tea and a nonfiction book. The scent of honeysuckle wafted from the bushes below and two kittens wrestled playfully beneath an empty porch hammock. Royal palm trees twice the height of the house rustled in the breeze constantly, reminding Grierson of the sound of turning newspapers. He sported a straw hat. His shirt, open at the neck, revealed his pale skin. His old baggy pants hung off him like a rag. He had lost weight but at least the colour was coming back to his face and his cough had stopped. He was smoking less. Here was a man no longer in a pressure cooker.

Energized by the surroundings, Grierson blustered, "The issue in democracy is to distinguish between two powerful groups. The political elite is elected, and by definition, will change periodically. The other group is the educators, the educated elite. No one elects them, who by virtue of their own talent and desire, stand above partisan politics. The educators are devoted to the idea of Democracy and State, and values that will benefit the whole of society."

Margaret interjected sweetly. "Now John, this all sounds like one of your undergraduate sermons. What about practical politics?"

Undeterred, Grierson continued, "As I see it, the really hard and disagreeable task of education tomorrow is that it will have, willy-nilly, to re-examine its attitude to such fundamental concepts as property and wealth, natural rights, and freedom of contract. It will have to think more cautiously when it comes to the word 'Opportunity' and the phrase 'Free Enterprise.' These concepts themselves will not be obliterated. They are simply due for a sea change, which will leave them somewhat different from what they were before."

"Yes, John," said Margaret, "but here in North America, everyone's dream is to have the world as their own oyster. How can you change *that*?"

He continued, "Positive thinking. We shall find new concepts coming more powerfully into our lives; and we shall dramatize them so that they become loyalties and take leadership of the will. We shall talk less of the world as everyone's oyster and more about work and jobs. We shall talk less about free enterprise and competition and more about the State as a partner in initiative. There will be less about liberty and more about duties; less about the past and more about the future. Already you hear the new words in the air: 'Discipline,' 'Unity,' 'Coordination,' 'Total Effort,' 'Planning.' They are the first swallows over the horizon; and there are going to be more of them…"

Margaret was unimpressed. "That's pretty heady stuff, dear. But surely you are talking about your one man crusade."

"I am not," Grierson replied. "I want to emancipate the citizens and salvage some sort of authentic democracy. If you cannot teach the citizenry to know everything about everything all the time, you can give them a comprehension of the dramatic patterns within a living society."

Neither he nor Margaret realized that he was anticipating media theorist Marshall McLuhan by some twenty years. McLuhan would call such patterns *myths*. Grierson, like McLuhan, understood that the two options for education were a simple reduction: to be for democracy and against authoritarianism or to be for authoritarianism.

"I tell you Margaret, one thing is sure, like those kittens tumbling under the hammock, freedom has to be fought for. Back in my university days, when Walter Lippmann pronounced practical democracy impossible, he was dead wrong when he said that informed elites were necessary to make the important societal decisions in the contemporary world, as well as to manufacture consent."

Grierson forgot he was sick and supposed to be in bed. He leaped to his feet, tossed his notepad on the chair, emptied his glass in a gulp, lit a cigarette and continued in his animated way. "The elites should act on behalf of the citizens, whose views they are obliged to reflect. If governments and industry have taken over the essence of the educational process in the name of propaganda, to stay honest, they have a moral obligation to share this power with professional educators and constitutional authorities."

"All right, John," Margaret said. "Calm down. The doctors said no more stress and bother."

But Grierson was just getting going. "This is not stress or bother. This is the Truth. Don't you see? Being a member of an elite means responsibility to serve the general public, not one's own interests. This calls for a special kind of individual in a North American culture that worships individualism and monetary success. I have been seeking out and hiring idealists who share this philosophy. These are the medicine men who have the hearts and determinations of teachers. They hope to teach people to *feel* things not to *know* things. The best people know they have been chosen by some higher power to use their gifts…"

"What power, dear? You?" she joked in her gentle manner, eyes twinkling.

"Don't be funny, Margaret. I mean that there is some kind of system operating in which a higher power has already chosen those who demonstrate His choice by doing selfless work on behalf of those who are not chosen."

"Sounds like Scots Presbyterianism to me," she laughed.

"Not at all. My practical knowledge of working class misery only strengthened my belief that I was put on this earth to show others the Right Way. I believe the God of Moses elected me to do His work."

"John, do you mean to say…" she sounded puzzled.

He realized he was on shaky ground. He decided to back peddle. "Being elect anyway, that is a falsehood."

And the conversation ended there. He spent the next few days scribbling furiously, then put down his pen and announced, "Margaret, it's time to get back to work in Ottawa." There was no time for a leisurely train. They took a plane.

∞

Back in the Ottawa snow, he met icy indifference and silence from the prime minister. Grierson was overworked running two agencies and frustrated with the government's slow response to his suggestions. He was disappointed to learn they intended to drop any reference to propaganda from the information services once war ended.

Late in December, another King insider took him aside privately and told him he was too far ahead of the government. King was not happy to see Grierson's focus shifting to a postwar and international context while Ottawa itself had not yet decided on policy. "Grierson, they are calling you a 'hot gospeller' on the Hill," he began. "Not a few are concerned with your brash manner and your preaching that government should continue to regulate daily life and inspire the citizenry with information. You know politicians want to stay in power more than they want to propagandize, good cause or not. You are stepping on a lot of toes."

Grierson saw the writing on the wall. He decided to resign when his contract expired in January. In spite of his bragging that he and King were almost pals, the fiery Scot had made too many enemies in Ottawa. King and company must have been glad to see Grierson return to the National Film Board and his first passion, documentary film. What he loved best was to skitter about and oversee his filmmakers. When it came to wartime film, Grierson was on a roll.

7

Public Servant at the NFB

It takes time and rest to recover from a physical breakdown, and not long after Grierson returned to Ottawa, he relapsed. Back home in his sickbed, he promised himself and Margaret to stop drinking. He drank only water for seven weeks. From bed, he continued to oversee much of the Film Board's daily operation, including hiring the creative staff. Sometimes he seemed eccentric, carrying on a monologue with an applicant for two hours or asking about painting or literature. He admitted to Margaret that his employment criteria were unusual. "Young people from the universities, preferably with degrees in the social sciences, are what Canada needs," he insisted. "Filmmaking

At his NFB moviola, Stuart Legg taught editing and writing skills
to young Canadian filmmakers. Editors wore white gloves
to protect the film while editing. Note the friendly eyes
of a Russian Allied soldier in the poster.

skills are the equivalent of learning how to shine boots and all that baloney. I am looking for young adults who know the country, who can feel its pulse."

One afternoon, surrounded by spilling folders and scattered newspapers on his bedcovers, he interviewed a recent graduate from the University of Toronto. Tom Daly may have seemed tentative and mystical, but he was blessed with a photographic memory, the sensibility of a poet, and a love of detail. Daly thought, *Now this is unusual indeed: a public servant working from his sickbed. I think the NFB is my kind of place to work.* Grierson offered him a six-month contract. He stayed forty-five years. Similarly did Stanley Jackson, a Winnipeg schoolteacher, arrive at the sickbed. After three interviews, he had said nothing while Grierson did all the talking. Something in Jackson's demeanour convinced the boss he was sensitive, alert, and poetic. Jackson became a formidable researcher and writer, and some of the Film Board's best postwar films reflected his narration skills. He also stayed four decades.

Grierson demanded personal loyalty above all else. In return, the staff had a sense that they were at the centre of all things Canadian. If he were happy with a completed film he might say to its creator, "You're the only one here who has *It.* You must light a torch for these other young talents and stick it under their rear-ends." Or he might dismiss a hard-wrought but dissonant piece with a curt, "It stinks."

Travel and talk were his preferred pastimes. He criss-crossed the continent frequently, learning about Canada all the while. He summed up this experience,

"Personal contacts are so easy in a small country with a small population. I remember drinking a bottle of gin with a Saskatchewan bank manager who then promised to show me an example of local horticulture. He drove me thirty miles outside of China, Saskatchewan to a forlorn tree standing in the middle of a grassy plain and said, 'Here's the local horticulture.' Strange sense of humour, or seriousness, these Canadians…"

Making a film is more than learning how to shine boots and Grierson knew it. He brought in artists from abroad to train the Canadians. Stuart Legg, his most capable talent, had been a Cambridge graduate and a gifted member of the EMB documentary film school in Britain. Legg passed on his editing skills to Tom Daly and taught him how to bring rhythm to images. From New York, Grierson invited Norman McLaren to form the animation department. He had met the young artist when judging the Scottish Amateur Film Festival in 1936 and was impressed by his animation method of painting directly onto celluloid. McLaren, a pacifist, first resisted Grierson's invitation, fearful he would have to make propaganda. Grierson told him he would have artistic freedom; his public service messages became instant classics. *Let's All Sing Together* and *Chants populaires* animated popular folk songs and went far to win the loyalties of English and French Canadians. McLaren, as both teacher and artist, put Canada on the map of world animation. Of Grierson, he enthused, "He protected the creative talents from outside pressures, encouraging the artists to grow and experiment freely. Most of all, he instilled in us the idea of the artist being a public servant."

Working for the NFB could be a brutalizing love-hate experience. Once, Grierson barged into a tiny office where the documentary team of five men and women was huddled around two racks of fifty pieces of film of varying sizes, shots waiting to be spliced together to make a coherent visual statement, and all for next week's deadline. He asked what they were doing. "A friendly argument about assembling these pieces to create the film's texture," answered a female editor.

"Texture? Haven't you been following basic rules? A film should clarify, synthesize, simplify, popularize and be spiritual." He then sat down on the floor with his legs crossed and spent the next twenty minutes haranguing them provocatively. There followed a contradictory remark that threw them all. "However, if you look at things this way..." and after another lecture, the whole session ended with a brief footnote on Immanuel Kant. "Now you see what I mean. Fix it..." he said, disappearing as quickly as he had arrived, never apologizing for taking up their precious work time. He had shown them light, and working on unpaid overtime, they finally got the texture and clarity right.

In another instance, he ordered consultant Paul Thériault to conduct a survey of the NFB's French-language film distribution in Quebec. "Have it on my desk in two months," snapped the tyrannical commissioner.

Thériault worked eighteen-hour days for the next two months to prepare a report he swore to Grierson was so accurate that he would bet his life on it.

Handing it over to him, he watched in horror as Grierson tore it up and dumped it in a basket. "Why you no good... if you weren't so short, I would knock you down," Thériault fumed.

"Take it easy young man. Now you know what is needed. I don't need to know. I already knew. From now on you are on your own. Implement the recommendations!"

Grierson knew he could trust him to set up a better Quebec distribution network. This kind of painful teaching hurt the student badly, but ultimately gave him the confidence to succeed.

Grierson continued to build and inspire a talented staff, whether from abroad or within Canada, whether men or women. In fact, women became the backbone of the organization, serving as stock shot researchers (jokingly called "pirates" for their ability to find shots), as editors, as writers, and as administrators. Grierson's progressive attitude to hiring women was laudable, but he took it personally if they left to marry. In one memorable fit of pique, following a female's admission that she was getting married, Grierson bellowed, "Ditched again by a friggin' woman. What do you do? You spend six, nine months, a year, training them and then they get up like bloody breeding cattle and walk off into the stable!" Such politically incorrect language only underscores how Grierson wanted his staff to give fully and selflessly in "the job of the century." He admitted that the women were stronger talents than the men, and he felt betrayed personally each time one left.

∞

The two most important series of the NFB were for cinemas, *Canada Carries On* and from 1942, *The World in Action.* Stuart Legg, as director, writer, and editor, pioneered both. His intelligence and language put flesh on to the skeleton of Grierson's film ideas. From the tremendous wealth of images that Legg called "Tolstoian," his filmmaking teams fashioned a visually compelling monthly screen editorial. In a pre-television age, the twenty-minute newsreel, shown in theatres just before the Hollywood feature, was how the public learned about contemporary events visually.

Not long after giving up his Wartime Information Bureau job, an edgy and exhausted Grierson banged into the editing room where Stuart Legg had been on his feet almost twelve hours, standing at a moviola on a workbench. The room was small and stuffy, about half the size of a regular room. There were no windows and all four walls were made from asbestos, to confine flames if an accidental fire broke out. Some wartime posters were the only colour. *Ce qu'il faut pour vaincre*, read one, showing a determined soldier charging into the fray, and "I was a victim of careless talk" read another, as a ghost face framed a ship sinking.

Legg, a tall, thin figure, was bent over the equipment. Always soft spoken, he seemed the epitome of an English country gentleman. His razor-sharp brain never failed to provide him with words to describe a moment or situation with precision. He wore white cotton gloves, the usual tool of an editor, to avoid getting fingerprints or dirt on the celluloid. An unsmoked cigarette lay burning in an ashtray as he cranked by hand a reel mounted on one end of the table, winding up the film from another reel connected to the other end. In the centre of the table was the moviola, a brightly lit magnified small screen through which the film passed as the operator cranked the handle and which showed the image as it would appear in the cinema.

His face haggard, he was on edge. So was Grierson. "Stuart, don't you remember anything about rhythm?" barked Grierson. In a rare moment of temper, Legg snapped back, "You missed the beat, John. I'm running the bleeding footage backwards." A seldom embarrassed Grierson mumbled a vulgarity and withdrew. Legg was angry that the boss had been away so long from moviemaking and had left him supervising the lion's share of the creative work.

∽

Canada Carries On and *The World in Action* were influenced by the American newsreel *The March of Time*, one of the main sources of visual news in North American cinemas. Legg had worked for the Americans before the war, and had learned to tailor the script to fit the images, many of which were stock shots gathered in New York and/or from around the world. As editor and writer, he was responsible for most of the creative energy behind the NFB newsreel-based product. The twenty-minute films were typically low key – didactic, earnest to the point of seriousness, and personal in their appeal. They never violated Legg's first documentary rule, "Thou shalt not be dull."

He wove three principle threads together, the visuals, the narration, and the music. Arguments had to be simple, clear and forceful, without appealing to raw emotions or reducing problems to bland clichés. The principal narrator, Lorne Greene, was skilled at recording in a commanding voice the whole film's narration, live, and without stopping. The words had to match each three-to-five-second shot. For example, a smiling downed Allied airman, being rescued and pulled from the sea "laughed in the face of Death." Similarly the NFB orchestra watched the images on a screen before them as they recorded the music track, starting with an initial crescendo and ending in a stirring major chord. Music created a sense of breathlessness.

The two series embodied Grierson's functional principle of modern propaganda: education, inspiration, and explanation of the patterns of total war. *Canada Carries On* appeared each month in eight hundred Canadian theatres, reaching four million viewers. Similarly *The World in Action* reached millions more in 6,500 U.S theatres. In a pre-television age, these newsreels put Canada into the world picture.

The films urged citizens to focus and find purpose in their collective energies. As well, they promised a postwar world minus the luxury of insularity and isolationism. Some items gave Canada a sense of national identity and pride as they focused on the potential of the North and of the future itself. They always provided consistency, hope, assurance, and direction. They also largely avoided racism while condemning fascism. Thus, while Hitler "the little painter from Austria" was fair game as an object of scorn, there was no name calling of the Germans or Japanese.

A frequent theme was that Canada's great strength was the individual's voluntary commitment to the struggle as part of a collectivity. Women received unprecedented recognition in numbers like *The Home Front, Proudly She Marches, Women Are Warriors,* and *Inside Fighting Canada.* As Grierson put it to an American reporter, "Film Board films are designed deliberately to promote a sense of national unity and a national understanding between the many groups which go to make the Canadian nation as well as to interpret Canada to the world at large." Both the *New York Times* and *Time* magazine applauded the NFB for its evenhandedness.

There were occasional problems. After the fall of Mussolini, the prime minister objected to *The Gates of Italy* for asserting that Italians were victims of Mussolini and the Germans. On the other hand, he approved of *The War for Men's Minds.* King was probably most impressed with its portrayal of him on an equal level with Roosevelt and Churchill. The public did not know that the U.S. and Britain excluded King from both wartime conferences in Quebec City. The prime minister was content to pose with the Allied leaders for the photo opportunity. As for the film's message predicting permanent government propaganda and a new internationalism, King was unhappy. Grierson thought he was carving his signature with Ottawa's blessing. Taken in by his own rhetoric, he failed to see that *The War for Men's Minds* was too wordy. It fell flat with audiences who preferred to see images of enemy planes falling out of the sky.

∞

If he was riding high as propaganda maestro, Grierson found himself a target for not going far enough with information on one hard-hitting wartime subject, the Holocaust. The Jewish genocide in Europe was no longer the rumour it had been since the fall of 1942. There were reports coming through the international press about the ongoing destruction of 400,000 of Hungary's Jewish population.

His best Jewish friend in Ottawa, Arthur "Killer" Gottlieb, was drinking with him in midsummer 1944 at the Chateau Laurier bar late one night just before closing. He became brave. "Grierson, you may be Mr. Ho-Presto Propaganda, but it is heartbreaking that the Film Board has maintained a virtual silence about Hitler's war against the Jews."

This caught the normally talkative Grierson off balance. There was uncharacteristic silence for a few moments as he glared angrily at his friend, sipped his gin, and smoked his cigarette. He was thinking of how his sister Ruby, evacuating British children on a transport ship a few years earlier, had been torpedoed by a German submarine and had drowned with hundreds of others. The death of innocent civilians never left him unmoved.

Finally he spoke. "We had some Nazi newsreel stuff that showed prewar anti-Semitism. But you know, there just is no contemporary footage about the rumours we keep hearing about mass killing of civilians."

"Come on Grierson, you know bloody well the killing machine against the Jews goes on unchecked," prodded the bold Gottlieb. "Let's face it. Canada is an anti-Semitic country that couldn't give a damn about the Jews."

"I'll tell you something about Canadian politics," the Scotsman replied testily. "The Liberal Government is willing to be led by, rather than to lead a Canadian public opinion that is frankly anti-Semitic, particularly in Quebec, where the Catholic Church continues to equate Jews with godless communism. We made an oblique gesture in 1943 to cover this emerging human catastrophe. We asked the question, 'Will the German people be held responsible for the mass deportations and killing and wounding of children?'"

"Yes I know," said Gottlieb. "But why didn't you mention the Jewish refugees?"

"Keep this under your hat, Killer," Grierson replied, "The Cabinet War Committee declared Canada's information policy on this issue: remain silent. Ottawa ordered all atrocity stories held up until they could be verified. How in Hell's name do we verify what's going on in the heart of Nazi Europe? Government policy has spared Canadian civilian morale and some possible guilt feelings. Mr. King's government has long depended upon Quebec's votes and seats in Parliament, and English Canada fears becoming awash in a sea of Jewish refugees. The government is not prepared to lose votes on the Jewish issue. It is a closed subject at the NFB."

Gottlieb was unimpressed. "Come on, Grierson, you have seen the American press. They estimate the final Jewish body count will be in the millions."

"Maybe, my friend. Maybe. I remember how propaganda in the First World War contained atrocity stories that proved to be invented or exaggerated. Look, the Jewish tragedy is a sideshow. Estimates of total war dead are already in the tens of millions. Besides, we and the Yanks are sensitive to German propaganda that continues to insist that the Jews are pulling the Allies' political strings. We have been told to forget this angle. Sorry, but I can only go as far as government sanction allows. The Jews are a closed subject. My powers, be they what they are, are limited." Grierson was distinctly uncomfortable.

His drinking partner was far from sober. He looked around the almost-empty room and whispered, "Well, I'm not trying to pull any strings, but I heard that you were a little anti-Semitic yourself at the Film Board." He continued belligerently, "Julian Roffman says that when some racists at the NFB called his production unit 'the Palestine Unit,' you defended those fascists and admitted there were too many Jews. And when Roffman protested there was only himself and one other, you barked, 'That's too many.'"

Grierson swallowed hard, not sure whether to tell Gottlieb to shut up or to explain the circumstances on that singularly bad day. He had fired Roffman's boss in a huff of anger, put young Roffman in charge, then changed his mind, and was trying to undo his hasty decision. He ended up insulting both artists.

The bartender announced "Last Call," and Grierson ordered two more gins. He downed one in a gulp. "You know very well I don't need to mouth a stupid cliché like, 'Some of my best friends are Jews.' Killer, you don't understand a thing about Canadian politics. I am in the hot seat right in the heart of

Canada's political centre. In spite of an 'arm's length' relationship with my patrons, I am not a free agent. I belong to no specific party, and describe myself as one inch to the left of the Party in power. I am a public servant who's bound by an unwritten sanction: Do not get too far ahead of the government. And instead of them telling me what I can and cannot do, 'arm's length' means I operate under self-censorship. I can't do anything about the Jews, period."

He had been caught in the ultimate bind. Grierson swallowed his last drink, aware once again that he had forgotten his sickbed pledge to quit drinking. To himself, he admitted he hated the "mediocrity of spirit" that he saw everywhere in the civil service around him. He was reaching a point where he was thinking of moving on, believing a new generation of Canadian filmmakers was ready to "take Canada to places it has never so far dreamed of..." Little did he know that his enemies could not wait to see him go. And the ambush that caught him was of his own making.

8

Victim of the Cold War

Impressive audience statistics justified Grierson's belief he was at the peak of success late in 1944. A nagging question remained: Once war ended, what place would there be for him? One King lieutenant dismissed his offer to head the Canadian Broadcasting Corporation (CBC). "Grierson is a dreaming outsider, clueless about internal Canadian politics, and is not practical. As I see it, he has an over appreciation of his efforts; his political masters have an under appreciation, which is as far below as is his above. The gap between the two is tremendous."

He had made enemies with permanent civil servants when he called himself "a temporary employee

Newsmen had a field day photographing alleged spies called before the postwar Royal Commission on Espionage in Government Service. A cruel coincidence drew Grierson into the web of suspicion, and his North American career crashed in flames.

who enjoys kicking things around." The inner circle around the prime minister detested his authoritarian operating style and bluntness. He had embarrassed several cabinet ministers when he reported, "Research has shown that there is a feeling in the country that there is a lack of vision and inspiration in Ottawa." If he was echoing polls, he was also burning bridges with adventurous policies.

One windy day in December 1944, Grierson was back in the Prime Minister's Office, testing the waters with King's secretary, Walter Turnbull. "Walter, should Canada pursue non-theatrical (documentary) film or try to form a feature industry of its own?" he queried.

Turnbull was silent, knowing that a lecture was about to begin. "From my vantage point," said the Scotsman, "for Canada to compete with monopolistic Hollywood is foolish. It flies in the face of the continental economic integration that the war has started. Further, a Canadian quota system limiting foreign films is impossible, because Ottawa would never go toe-to-toe with the U.S. on economic matters. Besides, each province guards *its* prerogative jealously to decide what will or will not be shown. Forget features. To me, documentary films are *the* authentic mass communicators because they are seen by the educated, the community opinion leaders, and social activists."

Turnbull smiled. "You don't really want my opinion, do you?"

Grierson pretended he did not hear. "We enjoy free distribution of Canadian travelogues in the U.S. Why kill the golden goose?"

"Don't forget the money, John," King's secretary offered.

"Of course not. I know we can do nothing to stop the outflow of eighteen million dollars a year profit to Hollywood, which calls us part of their domestic market. Yet Ottawa keeps eight million dollars in taxes. Why argue with that? Hollywood has a headlock on Canada and nobody in Ottawa wants an economic war against Hollywood, right?" Turnbull nodded in agreement. The case was closed. There would be no attempt to start a Canadian feature film industry until the 1960s.

∽

Japan surrendered in August 1945 and Grierson tendered his resignation. In a personal letter to the prime minister, he explained, "I want to do some pioneering before I slow up. I extend heartfelt thanks to you, Prime Minister, for your personal blessing to the NFB. I believe this has happened because I understood your mind, had your personal confidence and could rely on your generosity. I and Legg and a number of Film Board employees plan to form a private company in New York and to extend documentary production on an international level."

King waited until November to answer in a brief note. "I appreciated your efforts over the years, even though our contacts had been infrequent," he began. "Yet you were a friend who interpreted our aims and motives fairly." Meanwhile King refused the Film Board's recommendation that Grierson receive three months' salary as a going away gift. There was something discordant in this, but Grierson could not figure out if it was pettifogging on the part of Ottawa bureaucrats, the result of hostile persons settling scores, or something worse. It was something worse, much worse.

The Royal Canadian Mounted Police had information implicating Grierson and the NFB in a spy scandal that would coincide with the end of the Second World War and beginning of the Cold War. A Russian cipher clerk in the Soviet embassy in Ottawa, Igor Gouzenko, defected on September 6, 1945, and brought with him codes, files, and information concerning a Soviet spy ring operating in Canada. He handed over names of alleged agents, assignments, and directives from Moscow. Some agents worked for the Canadian government, and knew technical, as well as atomic energy secrets.

The prime minister was horrified that this affair could affect government peacemaking and even the world. At Laurier House, he sat alone beside his mother's painting while scratching notes into his diary. He had resumed attending séances where he had been speaking to her and Prime Minister Wilfrid Laurier, his own patron as a young politician, both dead these many decades. King wrote, "I want to drop out of public life at once to avoid the embarrassment this business will bring. I am convinced that Canada is honeycombed with communists." His mood swung from seeing himself as an instrument to help save the world, to despair over this unrelenting problem.

King was particularly worried that the arrangements being made for postwar settlements by the Big

Four (Allied Powers) might be destroyed. He even hoped the Americans would urge him to suppress the Gouzenko evidence. They did not. The Secretary of State told him, "Handle things your own way."

In part, the scandal revolved around the key question of whether to share the secret of the atomic bomb with the U.S.S.R. Late in October, King was discussing the issue with ex-Prime Minister Churchill and now Prime Minister Attlee of Britain. Churchill did not trust the Russians while Attlee, if less antagonistic, was taking his cue from President Truman in Washington. Ironically, President Roosevelt had been leaning towards sharing the secret prior to his sudden death in April 1945. Truman wanted to demonstrate his toughness to American officials as well as to the Soviets. He opposed sharing the bomb. The Washington Declaration in November 1945 reflected Truman's position: contain Russian expansionism so as to force the U.S.S.R. to modify itself. He called his policy one of firmness and patience. Coincidentally this fit in neatly with Canada's desire to maintain defence co-operation with the U.S. The Cold War had begun.

When the RCMP began verifying the Gouzenko evidence, several sensational allegations emerged. There were agents in National Research and External Affairs, a Member of Parliament might be involved, and a Film Board employee was connected with the main spy ring. She had been Grierson's secretary for six months from May to November 1944. Her work was evidently unsatisfactory to Moscow and they wanted her to undertake scientific work in the National Research Council (NRC) with another agent, to learn the formulae for RDX explosive. It was supposed that Grierson would help her get a new position at the NRC, which happened to be the next office over from his.

Grierson had no inkling of the contention that he was in touch with spies and communists. He was wondering why the prime minister seemed to have no interest in choosing someone to succeed him at the NFB. King was silent. To his diary, King confided, "I have been suspicious of his [Grierson's] sympathies with communism, etc. Grierson's name appears in the evidence as one who clearly was in touch with the head of the [Soviet] military organization here and with other Communists. I had always been a little concerned about what he was doing in regard to contact with the leading Communist elements at the Russian embassy... The whole situation at the Film Board needs looking into as there is reason to believe there is quite a Communist nest there." King warned the minister in charge of the Film Board not to let Grierson influence his choice of successor, even if it was the prime minister's old loyalist, Ross McLean.

Another King lieutenant felt morally certain that Grierson knew nothing of his secretary's connection with the Soviet spy ring. King was convinced otherwise, and thought communism was a low-grade infection, a communist germ. He told one confidant, "The Film Board's personnel are too radical politically and I now remember with regret the few films that had caused ripples."

The hapless Grierson had no idea he was being hung out to dangle in the wind. The Gouzenko evidence remained secret until February 1946 when word was leaked in Washington. King then ordered the appointment of a Royal Commission (Taschereau-Kellock Commission) to investigate allegations of espionage in government service.

Summoned from New York City, Grierson appeared as a witness in April and May. The council chambers were packed with onlookers and the non-circulating air became stuffy after an hour. When presented with Gouzenko's evidence, he denied any connection between himself and his secretary's alleged scheming to get promoted to the National Research Council. He said, "She came to me as a secretary from the International Labour Organization and worked for me for half a year." He concluded, "I merely think of her now as an ambitious girl who certainly wanted to get on in terms of the Film Board."

The counsel for the Commission asked him if he knew any officials at the Russian Embassy. Grierson replied, "I knew people at the diplomatic level, but the Russians were 'correct,' that is, they never intimated that they would like someone promoted to the NRC." He had nothing to help the Commission. But they were not done with him. He made a gesture to get up to leave, but the lawyer said, "Just a moment Mr. Grierson. We have a few more questions." He was hoping to learn about left-wing study groups, but Grierson, now suspicious of his interrogator, did not take the bait. When asked about the existence of study groups at the NFB, he said there were all kinds of such groups, usually incidental and casual, dealing with bilingualism, nutrition, health, town planning, rural sociology, and so forth.

The counsel probed deeper, asking if Grierson knew two individuals who worked at the Wartime Information Board, where he had been boss. "Yes," he offered, "One, a professor, was sentimental left-wing rather than actively political."

"But you knew the professor was a communist sympathizer, didn't you, Mr. Grierson?" queried the lawyer.

"No," Grierson replied, "The man was a left-wing sympathizer and friend of the U.S.S.R., but not a communist sympathizer."

The counsel asked about another WIB employee. Grierson said, "The man was more social democrat than active Communist Party member." He did not realize he was walking into a trap.

He returned to testify in May. The room was packed to overflowing with curious onlookers. Grierson was uneasy with the undercurrent of murmuring and wondered if this was what it was like in the days when hanging was still public entertainment.

He did not expect the first question to be so direct, "Why did you select the left-wing sympathizer over another more qualified man?"

Grierson denied this, claiming he did not know the man's political leanings in 1943. The lawyer took a direct line of attack and then asked him bluntly, "...Are you a communist or communistically inclined?"

The normally unflappable Grierson was shocked. His facial expression shifted from surprise to anger. He decided to lecture the young lawyer. "Young man, I have been first and last a public servant, that is a civil servant. It is one's duty to press as far as possible for progressive legislation, but within firm and very strict rules… In the matter of political philosophy the issue is this: those of us who have been trained and who are dyed-in-the-wool Liberal democrats say there cannot be any economic freedom if there is no political freedom. On the other hand, those who believe in international socialism say there cannot be any political freedom unless there is economic freedom."

The counsel was not impressed with the political science lesson. He then asked bluntly, "Are you a member of the Communist Party?"

Grierson answered, "Oh no."

The lawyer parried, "Would you say then that your inclinations were of the leftist variety?"

An indignant Grierson replied, "I am entirely a person who is concerned with the establishment of good international understanding. Therefore I am concerned with the floating of all ideas. I mean, I get as much from Gobineau [a nineteenth-century racist] as I get from Marx."

This reply did not convince the chief commissioner, who accused him of knowingly hiring communists. Further, he insisted, "This Commission has uncovered the existence of an astonishingly large number of communist cells masquerading as study groups… and an astonishingly large number of persons working in those cells and drawing other people into them were employees of the Film Board…"

Denying the accusation, Grierson replied, "The atmosphere at the NFB was one of progressive, not leftist, thought."

Another lawyer pushed further, insisting, "The Russian evidence shows in almost every case that persons named were communists or tied up with the communists or communist sympathizers..."

Flummoxed, Grierson denied the allegation, and the counsel sprung the trap. He insisted that the Russians meant to have Grierson put his secretary in the National Research Council "because we know that Grierson belongs to this clan, or we know he will do it for us..."

When the unhappy witness suggested, "My secretary might merely have intended to manipulate the boss because I was her boss," it sounded lame. The interrogation was over as he concluded that she resigned from the Film Board after being refused a raise, then vanished. He had answered the Commission's questions with typical honesty, if too much like a schoolteacher. ("Much too clever," said one friendly observer.) After all, the professionals were pursuing their appointed task of investigating, and the result was that he now looked suspect.

Those close to the government thought he had been indiscreet and careless, but in politics, where appearances are everything, that can be as bad as being guilty. To illustrate, on the day after his testimony in Ottawa, Grierson addressed the International Conference of the Junior League on the implications of the atomic bomb. The hall was almost empty. He suggested that as much as the Soviet Union was secretive, suspicious, and conspiratorial, the West had given them reason to be just that. "Any attempt to understand Russia becomes the badge of subversive activity," he insisted. "Mankind would never be saved if church or state frustrated and stifled the generous thoughts of our youth to learn the ideas operating in the world today, be they from Russia, Rome or from George Bernard Shaw." When he finished, there was almost inaudible applause.

Still fuming about being trapped in his testimony the day before, and having finished a half bottle of gin, he sat at the Chateau Laurier bar. There he wrote a letter telling the government that the Royal Commission was a direct threat to three of the four freedoms: freedom from fear, freedom of speech, and freedom of conscience. "If confidence were restored between Canada and the United Nations," he charged, "It would not be possible for the filthy insects and worms to creep out of the woodwork and reveal themselves again for their bigotry and prejudice and evil will. If these vicious things were permitted to continue without being repudiated, there would be nothing but the growth of suspicion, doubt and animosity between individuals, organizations and communities in the state."

Luckily, he did not send this angry alcohol-fuelled note. The government had been embarrassed, and though one or two ministers offered a halfhearted word on his behalf, most were happy to see him gone. Nobody spoke up publicly on his behalf. If the silence were not enough, in a final insult, Ottawa refused to reimburse his travel costs for a January 1946 trip from Britain to Canada to help maintain staff morale at the Film Board during the transition period. At last, the writing on the wall was comprehensible: John Grierson's Canadian career was over.

He never wrote or spoke publicly about his hurt, but in 1948 he summarized his feelings while finishing a contract for UNESCO in Paris. "I love Canada, even if it is a country that is not very knowledgeable about political philosophy or law. It is crude in parliamentary debate and has too many roosters crowing on local editorial dunghills."

He grew more angry as he remembered the shoddy treatment he had received. "Its public life lacks courage and Canada is the village that voted the earth was flat, in the denial of its size and destiny... Its educational standards are in many quarters grotesque and, in some quarters, subject to a species of provincial fascism which is both ignorant and vicious."

Yet he had a soft spot for that big lummox of a country. "Whatever positive there is to be found is in its libraries and adult education services. But Canada is a great bore when it tries to show sophistication. In spite of all that, there is a profound element of common sense and good taste about Canada and Canadian life which is a precious thing to know." He could not help but adore the gangly Canada like a parent loves a teenager.

These love-hate thoughts may have defined Canada of the forties, but Ottawa's politicians did not care if their silence and negligence left him to fall flat on his face. There were no bon voyage parties for John Grierson.

∞

Before leaving Canada, Grierson had a farewell drink with his longtime colleague Stuart Legg. He felt jilted that Canada could have abandoned him on such flimsy grounds. "I just don't understand it Legg," he said ruefully. "After all I have done for Canada how could the prime minister have abandoned me? I mean, my life feels like a matte projection."

Legg was puzzled. "What do you mean, a matte projection?"

"Well," Grierson continued, "It's like my life is happening on this giant sound stage, but behind me there is a whole other series of events being projected that I cannot even see."

"Oh, yes. That is a clever metaphor." Legg peered at his downcast friend. He had never seen Grierson so discouraged. It was as if a great light was diminishing.

Legg, ever the cool intellectual who had made a career of avoiding, rather than seeking the spotlight, could only agree. "This is a rotten deal." They continued drinking. Perhaps they had had one drink too many.

"Canada is a strange country, even niggardly when it comes to recognizing outsiders like ourselves who have given so much and have asked for so little," Legg commiserated.

Grierson took a last gulp of his drink and said, "Legg, I am going to say something I have never told anyone else before, and if you repeat it, I'll deny it to my dying day. Those cursed politicos in Ottawa are like a pig who eats her own farrow."

Legg blinked hard, his angular head cocked to one side. He was seeing a side of Grierson that had always been hidden. He ran his long fingers through his thinning blond hair. He tried using natural political savvy to ease the pain. "John, you are living proof that though the politically strong may not always be in the right, the politically weak are invariably in the wrong. Forget it. Let's show Canada our backsides."

9

Vagabond in the Dark

S tuart Legg and a host of other Film Board employees followed Grierson to New York. The bustle of
that great postwar metropolis should have generated
the energy to light up their new enterprise. Instead it
brought disaster. It was as if an unseen malevolent
hand was hexing everything. As Grierson arranged
financing, distribution, production, and sponsorship of
documentaries, strange things happened. On the same
day, his phone rang with the worst news. The Film
Board and Hollywood backed out of their distribution
deals. A week later, a telegram arrived telling him key
investors were being investigated as subversives by the
FBI. Funding stopped.

One permanent feature of Grierson's legacy was the NFB's national distribution network of films for Canadian schools. Here, at the Thora School near Orillia, the NFB rural agent for Ontario questions children on a film they have just seen.

From Canada, one disaffected ex-Film Board employee had been busy writing letters to the FBI, confirming that the boss was a communist. No one bothered to check the man's credentials. Grierson had fired him for being mentally unstable. As a dog jumps on a bone, the FBI began looking closely at everything and everyone connected to Grierson. In his Manhattan office, his mail arrived already opened. Answering the phone, he heard the static of someone listening in. Within two months, all his loyal disciples had to abandon him. The money was gone.

In Ottawa, where the FBI operated out of the U.S. embassy, they had passed on to Washington conflicting messages with a straight face: Grierson had fascist tendencies as well as communist sympathies and was in contact with subversives. Cold War paranoia was infectious. From the Ottawa embassy, the U.S. ambassador wrote a top secret letter to the Secretary of State in Washington. "I urge that no visa of any kind be granted to John Grierson until he is investigated and cleared." The letter was forwarded to FBI chief J. Edgar Hoover. The ever-suspicious Hoover, certain of Reds under almost every bed, was happy to oblige. He released the hounds.

Once the story of his visa refusal appeared in Canadian newspapers, Grierson's enemies smelled blood. The Opposition enjoyed embarrassing the Government, which abandoned their former servant. When he returned to Ottawa to try to mend fences, several reporters caught him leaving the politicians' elite Rideau Club. He had just been turned away as if he had soiled their plush carpets. Grierson defended himself with a limp explanation, "I am not a

Communist and any inference of this kind is ridiculous. The whole thing is silly, since I have been a British public servant for years." His words rang hollow. The insinuation and suspicion now infecting North America sealed his fate. He was alone, a pariah and a vagabond.

King's Minister of Justice, Louis Saint-Laurent, spoke up at last on Grierson's behalf. "I deplore the loose ill-founded conclusions pointing to Mr. Grierson as head of the spy ring or as consciously connected with it in any way," he ventured. But an avalanche, once started, cannot be stopped. The game was over when conservative minded Albertans called for censorship of NFB films. The federal Minister of Agriculture pointedly named two professed communists at the NFB. Two other provincial politicians lashed out at the agency's "moral depravity, gangsterism, and Communist propaganda."

It was hard to believe so many doors had closed. Old cronies refused to see him, officials did not keep their appointments, and one brave friend agreed to meet with him only at night and next to a public phone booth two blocks from Parliament Hill.

"It feels as if I am in a bad Hollywood movie," Grierson confided.

"You have no idea," his friend replied, looking around furtively to see if they were being watched. "Anyone seen with you is tainted. My advice is to get out of town." A dark figure in a doorway across the street lit a cigarette. Panicked, the friend wheeled about and sprinted away. Looking back over his shoulder he shouted, "Gotta go now," and disappeared into the blackness.

There was one last straw. Early in 1947 Grierson accepted the offer of a UNESCO plum post: adviser with special responsibility for mass media and public relations. The FBI's J. Edgar Hoover had other plans. Continuing his harassment, he wrote to the U.S. Attorney General that Grierson's presence in the U.S. was a threat to national security. He called a new agent into his office and told him "Talk to the *Washington Post*. Make sure they understand our position. Grierson is as pink as a carnation and would sooner be Red than dead." The director's words carried menace and the agent, believing the current rumour that an unhappy Hoover could mean a transfer to Nebraska, briefed the press fully and elaborately. Soon, a damning article appeared in Washington with the headline "Spy Suspect Gets UN Job."

Blissfully ignorant of these machinations, Grierson returned to Britain and Margaret. In London, he stopped at the U.S. embassy in Berkeley Square to pick up his visa for New York and the UN job. He waited for two hours. At last, a dour-faced consular official appeared, Grierson rose, but the man did not ask him into his office. He approached the exasperated Scot. "We have learned through our consulate in Montreal that the American government has refused your request for a visa," he said. Grierson thought he looked self-satisfied.

"What is the meaning of this?" he thundered. "I have a letter here offering me a United Nations posting that affords me diplomatic immunity. There must be some mistake."

"Sorry, Mr. Grierson. You are unable to qualify for a visa under our existing laws. There is no appeal.

There is to be no further inquiry." For the first time, the man smiled. Grierson's North American dream had turned into a nightmare straight out of Kafka's *The Trial*. He could only think of the story's last words: "Like a dog…" he kept repeating as he staggered into the London fog. He felt like a victim of unseen forces, about to be executed with the nonchalance of unfeeling people about to shoot a dog.

After weeks of knocking on doors and using every contact he had in Britain to protest, he waited with Margaret at their home, a cottage in Wiltshire, England, for a resolution. At last, a messenger arrived with an official letter from the United Nations. It was postmarked Geneva. Tearing it open expectantly, Grierson read it aloud to his wife. Disappointment again. He was not going to New York. "UNESCO is pleased to announce your appointment as adviser with special responsibility for mass media and public relations. You will occupy this post with full diplomatic status for a term of one year. Please report to our Paris offices on the Avenue Kléber in two weeks. Best of luck, Julian Huxley, Director."

∽

Grierson had been drinking heavily since 1946 and was nearly out of control emotionally in Paris. He tried to pick up the pieces at UNESCO, but was unsuited for the bureaucratic job. He haunted the corner of a well-known Parisian bar, the Columbia, opposite UNESCO headquarters at the Hotel Majestic on Avenue Kléber. The hotel's façade was still pockmarked from the fighting in 1944 that liberated Paris. He imagined the bullets were still flying, and his Canadian wounds had not healed. His gallows humour told of an inner hurt, "I always sit in the corner so no one can stab me in the back."

When sober, he tried to put on his best face, hoping he might set up systems in underdeveloped countries to promote education and train mass media people. As he put it publicly, "We must light up the imagination of people with a belief in themselves and in each other. To light up men's minds we need illuminating ideas... My stuff is where things are beginning and expanding."

Privately, Paris was not his milieu in spite of its inviting bars and bistros. The Columbia's bartender, an expatriate Briton, said with a shrug, "That unhappy Scotsman resembles a caged lion, ever restless, proselytizing zealously to any who drift in to listen. But few do."

In truth, Grierson missed documentary film and would do anything to return to his first love. Then, out of nowhere, a miracle. Robert Fraser, the director-general of Britain's Central Office of Information (COI), sent his secretary to Paris to invite Grierson to return to British documentary and carry out a new and bold approach to his agency's film operation. On paper, it looked like Fraser was offering him a British version of the National Film Board.

Grierson relished the return to London. His first day on the job was another letdown. The organization was situated in a faceless, nondescript five-storey office building of one hundred windows. And to his surprise, he learned that the COI had no status. It had no government minister in charge, nor could it make policy.

"So what in God's name am I supposed to do?" he asked Fraser, who kept staring out his window as if he were waiting for a ship to come in.

"We provide a common service to all departments. They will finance our films and tell you what they need. You get the fellows to make films to their order and liking," Fraser said. To boost the Scotsman's spirit, he spun round in his chair, surveyed his paper-filled desk, and concluded, "Only you can give us a new and bold approach. It's up to you, Old Boy. Cheers."

Grierson soon learned they had sold him a bill of goods. They were using him to oversee major cuts in funding and personnel. He said, "My job was to plan production and distribution of British government films. Instead, I taste dust in my throat, and like an old dog, am loved and tolerated, but expected to stay quiet in a corner while they pillage and burn."

After a year Grierson had lost his fire and thunder. Fraser called him into his office to complain. "The COI is top heavy with staff and unused facilities," he began.

"Not my doing," the intrepid Grierson complained. "That's what I inherited when I got here."

Still staring out the window, the director continued, "Nonetheless, overhead costs are excessive. Private companies can make the same films at a fraction of the price. Here are your marching orders in two words." He wheeled about in his executive chair, rose, and put his arm around Grierson's shoulder as he walked him to the door. "Slash costs," he said. He had handed the hangman his axe.

Grierson lost patience with the job and the bureaucracy. When the Conservatives won the 1951 general election, one of their first acts was to disband the COI Crown Film Unit. Not long after, Grierson met Stuart Legg in central London at the Reform Club, a private nineteenth-century establishment founded by the Liberal Party, where Legg was a member. Comfortable dark leather seats encouraged them to gaze up at the spectacular skylight in the open central area and think of a long gone, glorious era. Legg was doing some commercial work for a British firm, but was planning to quit documentary filmmaking and write a book on geopolitics, linking geography to history and conquest.

He looked at his friend, gaunt and drawn, who said, "Legg, being a civil servant's civil servant is not really my strength. I blame both the sponsors and the filmmakers at the COI. A whole new generation of filmmakers is anxious to replace this aging father of documentary. What can I do? I have no access to ministers, let alone the prime minister, and while the government plans to change the structure of British society, it has no time for documentary's approach to social reform."

Legg replied, "John, they stand ready to condemn the Father, his sermons, and his Son, the movement. I have heard that your harangues sound impressive and exciting at first, but they soon seem monotonous. At least in Canada, the documentary movement has redefined itself. Here in Britain, the Father lives, but the Son is all but dead. If I were you, I would pull the plug and quit." The exhausted Grierson had lost the will to fight. He agreed, and soon after, tendered his resignation.

∞

The rolling stone gathered no moss. Grierson had learned through the grapevine that the British government was putting public funds into a feature film experiment called Group 3. John Baxter, who was a gentle, soft-spoken, self-effacing, experienced studio director, invited him for lunch, which became a four-hour pitch to become an executive producer there. "John, we are hoping you could turn on the Grierson flair, fire, and brimstone. We want you to help attract young talent to direct films that will be documentary in texture, realistic in style, shot on location, and with an awareness of social democratic issues."

The reluctant Grierson replied, "I'd be the first to admit I am an odd choice, with no experience in studio production." Baxter plied him with another drink. "But I know you are sincere, Baxter. I'll do what I can to help launch the enterprise."

"One more thing, John. The films must definitely be fiction."

Here was a twist. Grierson had doubts about marrying documentary and fiction, in spite of the Italians' recent success with a style they called "neorealism." Maybe, just maybe, he could produce something as profound and earth shattering as Vittorio de Sica's *Bicycle Thieves*.

The only shattering was the mirror of expectations. The outcome of the Group 3 enterprise was a series of twenty-two experimental films, most of which were met with public indifference and poor distribution. Grierson was given responsibility as producer for nine productions, one of which was the critically acclaimed *The Brave Don't Cry*. In retrospect, most Group 3 films failed because the commercial industry feared and hated them.

By spring 1953 Grierson's smoker's cough worsened. Margaret told him, "John, if you don't see a doctor about that cough, I am going to pack you into an ambulance personally." This time he did not resist, because he knew something was wrong. The last time he was in London's polluted air, he could hardly breathe.

They took X-rays at the clinic and told him to wait. The afternoon dragged on. At last, a dour young doctor in a lab coat entered the waiting room with clipboard in hand. "He reminds me of an undertaker," growled the impatient Scot to Margaret.

He was not far off the mark as the intern brought him The Warning. "Mr. Grierson, your diagnosis is simple and severe. You have tuberculosis in both lungs. You must stop all work and agree to follow our regime or you will be dead in four months." He was not going home. He had punished his body to the limit and now had to pay for its abuse.

The reckless Grierson had a constitution of iron. Released months later, he spent the next year recuperating at the cottage in Wiltshire. While convalescing, he enjoyed puttering in the garden, where he raised colossal strawberries. Inactivity was simply not in his vocabulary. He continued commenting on story ideas and scripts for Group 3, which closed in 1955. Grierson offered a last bit of advice to the sputtering experiment. Thinking of the golden years in Canada, he said, "There is more artistic freedom for publicly funded socially motivated filmmakers than for feature filmmakers." No one listened to the lone vagabond in the dark.

10

This Wonderful World

G rierson was unemployed and broke. He owed the government years of back taxes, and ignoring his recovery from TB, he resumed drinking and smoking. The mid-fifties were his darkest years. "I am living on crumbs in Scotland, where I advise the Films of Scotland Committee," he groused to a Canadian friend. "I have been writing features about contemporary documentary film."

The truth was that Grierson missed Canada. In the spring of 1957 he accepted invitations to Vancouver, Edmonton, Toronto, and Montreal. In Toronto, several former Film Board employees invited three hundred people to fete their former

Grierson's television show educated and entertained.
"Use the experience of seeing things to look, think, and feel.
Today, it is the artists among us who brighten lives
and give zest and spirit to the people."

boss to make up for his humiliating departure in 1946.

In Montreal, he had the happy opportunity to see that the only offspring he ever fathered, the National Film Board, was now occupying a new, sprawling 5.25 million dollar complex in suburban St. Laurent. Its departing commissioner, the New Brunswick academic Albert Trueman, was to head the new Canada Council, a body to underwrite and protect Canadian culture. Invited to the farewell party, Grierson arrived late and not altogether sober. He bellowed across the room, "Trueman what's the crazy idea of leaving an important organization like the Film Board with its influence and cultural possibilities to go and take a measly administrative job and become the director of that money-giving bordello, the Canada Council?" Colleagues of the austere Trueman saw the tall, rigid, silver-haired academic mortified, then angry at his irascible guest. They had to restrain him physically from thrashing Grierson.

If he knew he had ruined the party, Grierson said nothing. He met the incoming film commissioner, Guy Roberge, a tall, portly, bespectacled, and congenial man from a family of French Canadian jurists, who in contrast to Grierson, radiated calm and reflection. Uninvited, Grierson offered advice. "Keep your office door open to your employees." Roberge did this, and not only stayed close to his staff, but also set the tone of the new era by stating anyone could write a memorandum in either French or English and it was up to the recipient to understand it. Official bilingualism came to Canada a decade later.

Grierson held court in the new facility. Surrounded by a half-dozen eager men and women in the NFB cafeteria, where the strongest beverage was coffee, he inspired and motivated a new generation. They did not mind him waxing enthusiastic: "The new Montreal headquarters is less important than seeking out far horizons. You have a magnificent, sprawling studio nearly four thousand miles long, containing a variety of scenic beauty and people to record. Get off your butts, stop gazing at your navels and capture on film what is authentic *today*, not yesterday."

He was ecstatic about the recent work of a small coterie of NFB filmmakers in Unit B. "The greatest single thing about the Film Board is its genius for portraiture, making pictures about individual people," he continued with usual conviction. "In *Paul Tomkowicz: Street-railway Switchman*, a solitary Polish immigrant goes through his nightly routine of clearing snow off trolley tracks in downtown Winnipeg. It is a visual tableau of contrasting blacks and whites against a backdrop of authentic street sounds and the simple plunking of balalaika strings," Grierson enthused. "This ten-minute short achieves lyrical height. The immigrant's isolation is magnified by the physical demands of Canadian winter and the single light he carries through the blustery night. Think of his comments about life he left in Poland: soldiers coming to his village and shooting his brother, sister and relatives… the human tragedy becomes a universal portrait. The alienated immigrant, separated tragically from family and roots, faces barriers of snow, windows, and language. In spite of all, he enjoys his Canadian freedom." They listened, transfixed. "Success in documentary is all about finding what common people everywhere can share sincerely," he concluded.

Later, he met with the Montreal head of CBC Television at the bar of the newly opened Queen Elizabeth Hotel in downtown Montreal, about six blocks from the Canadian Broadcasting Corporation studios. He tried to make a pitch for a CBC-Film Board marriage. "Look, it is well known that cinema audiences are declining, and you folks at CBC Television can benefit by helping the NFB reach more Canadians. Why can't both agencies become closer partners?" he urged.

The manager, who had come from CBC Radio, was respectful of the renowned documentary founder, but cautious. "In 1952, the year television came to Canada, there was an NFB-CBC agreement to show more films on television," the manager began. "It was a marriage made in hell. The Film Board acted like film and television were oil and water. They loathe television's unbending deadlines, time, sponsor, and editing constraints. Worst of all, they fear being absorbed by the ten-times-larger CBC. We have a weekly NFB news show, but no one thinks much of productions shot from the back of a station wagon."

The CBC executive did not reveal another secret: Producers at the CBC ignored NFB productions because there were no job promotions for helping outsiders. "Radio-Canada has better possibilities for the French side at the NFB," he continued. "They are in constant need of new material and don't have the resources to fill all the television hours in a week." The CBC-NFB marriage was never consummated.

∽

Grierson left for Scotland knowing that winds of change were blowing in Canada. By fall, 1957 he was far from it all, working on Scottish television. He had been known to bad mouth the medium: "Television at birth showed the promise of a genius, but grew up to be an idiot." When given the chance, however, he set out to find documentary a new home. He hosted a weekly television programme from Glasgow called *This Wonderful World* on a channel owned by Scots-Canadian newspaper tycoon Roy Thomson. He featured excerpts from worldwide documentary films on subjects as varied as aesthetics, science, music, and bullfighting.

The programme was an instant hit and soon he was his old bubbling self. On one show, he preached, "Use the experience of seeing things to look, think, and feel. The Church once had an exclusive duty to look after the mind, imagination, and spiritual welfare of a relatively primitive society. Today it is the artists among us who brighten lives and give zest and spirit to the people."

After each show, Grierson left the set at the Theatre Royal and headed for his favourite haunt, the Highlander Pub, just around the corner. There he sat high on a barstool (for height and authority), often continuing his fascinating lectures to his acolytes and friendly critics. He complained about problems with documentary style. "Today, filmmakers prop themselves up on barstools and take in each other's mental washing. This has taken the creative force out of the documentary process." He was thinking of his recent experience at film festivals in Cannes, Venice, and Edinburgh.

"The only brilliant productions I found were *Corral* and *City of Gold*, both from Canada. *Corral* is a little poem about man and the perpendicular, evoked by a single rider against the sky. It is the archetypal Canadian metaphor about time and space. It reveals the real life of the contemporary Alberta cowboy in idyllic, mythic images that celebrate horsemanship," he enthused. "The hero accommodates himself to Nature rather than conquers it, as he rounds up a herd of wild horses, lassoes one in the corral, then takes a wild plunging ride against a backdrop of the Rocky Mountain foothills. It is pure visual poetry that deserved first prize at the Venice Film Festival."

Grierson also loved *City of Gold*, a brilliant portrait consisting of some one hundred glass plate negatives of the Yukon Gold Rush of 1900. He remarked perceptively, "This twenty-one-minute film is not about those who found gold, but about that cluster of humanity around Dawson that never did. They reveal the secret of the North, the secret of Canada. Those luckless American and Canadian adventurers had found *community*, because the harsh climate made them dependent on each other. They needed each other (if you break a leg you have a friend) and discovered the secret of community, of love." In these brief comments, listeners marvelled at Grierson's undiminished ability to find the aesthetic heart of a film.

One evening, Grierson was on his customary way to the pub after a show that had featured soccer. He had elaborated upon it from an entirely new angle. "See it in terms of space, patterns in space, beautiful twisting and turning movements, changing and interchanging to bring a single green rectangle dramatically alive – just like the great painters tried to do."

As he approached the door, a scruffy, broad-chested Goliath stepped out of the pub, his rumpled working-class clothes signalling potential trouble. The man in the cloth cap recognized him and exclaimed earnestly, "Doc, that show tonight... Football and Leonardo da Vinci... I can only say one thing – it was friggin' poetry." For years, Grierson claimed this moment was the greatest homage he had ever received for his television work.

When *This Wonderful World* began broadcasting in Britain from 1959, Grierson thrilled to find it rocket to the top ten British television shows. To an enquiring reporter he claimed, "Showing films that are beautiful, brave, illuminating or inventive is not about teaching anybody or anything. The mere indication of what you believe to be beautiful or brave or inventive or illuminating or great may be enough to start in others a chain reaction of their own." To his mind, the greatest thing about good television was imagining a family arguing the pros and cons of a show and enlightening each other. Ever the teacher, Grierson enjoyed reaching his congregation of four to seven million members weekly from his television pulpit. *This Wonderful World* continued for ten years.

∞

In Canada in 1964, the National Film Board prepared to celebrate its twenty-fifth anniversary and invited its founder to deliver the keynote address. The microphone and old age dwarfed him physically, yet his sharp grey-blue eyes were like two beacons that seemed to flash on every filmmaker in the auditorium. His authoritative voice with its Scottish burr was as arresting as it had been a quarter century earlier.

While many artists expected the usual cheerleading from Grierson, there was some shock as he began his remarks, "The first principle of documentary – and it must be the first principle because I wrote it – is that you forget about yesterday. The only good film is the one you are going to make tomorrow." He was purposely deflating their "art for art's sake" egos. He reminded them of his core belief that the Film Board's relationship with Ottawa was the most precious affiliation it had. Knowing that their work was in the national interest is what gave the staff a sense of satisfaction. "To be a creative person at the Film Board," he concluded, "is the privilege to be a great public servant."

His words had small effect on a new generation of filmmakers. The Film Board had increased its staff in preparation for the audiovisual bonanza that became Expo 67, the Montreal World's Fair, in the approaching Centennial Year. And the current mania was to make Canadian features. But two formidable barriers were funding and distribution.

The ex-film commissioner trotted out his old argument. "Theatrical distribution is mainly in American hands, and few now or ever will see Canadian features. The government could face parliamentary embarrassment for squandering taxpayers' money on expensive failures." He concluded, "Let's face it, a feature is a long shot, and it is unfair to ask a minister to defend a long shot in Parliament."

If filmmakers heard him, they did not listen. Many hated making films for government departments, calling the work "plumbers' jobs." Meanwhile the private sector, wanting government support, lobbied to shut down the NFB. The Film Board needed friends and a mission statement, or the public might think it was obsolete.

∞

There was a profound change beginning to convulse French Canadian society. After the death of Quebec's autocratic premier Maurice Duplessis in 1959, a virtual dam had burst, and a deluge of intellectual, artistic, and political light cascaded over French Canada.

Grierson met with a number of the French-speaking filmmakers who were turning away from the documentary style called *cinéma vérité* or direct cinema. "We want a filmmaking style that reflects the new *prise de conscience* percolating through Quebec," said Gilles Groulx, one radical filmmaker who echoed clichés about decolonization, working class solidarity, and Marxism.

"Surely you must be aware of the limits," argued Grierson. "Listen to some of your best intellectuals like Pierre Trudeau and Gerard Pelletier. They despise the idea of French Canadian nationalism. They say it means retreat into a shell, and death from stagnation and suffocation. Trudeau calls Quebec nationalists politically reactionary *petit bourgeois* intellectuals, flapping their arms in ignorance."

"What does he know?" spat Groulx. "A millionaire's son with a golden spoon."

Grierson hated this kind of argumentation. "I don't see what is wrong with his idea of challenging French Canadians to show themselves as equals with the rest of Canada, not to be excluded from it."

"You don't get it, Grierson. This issue will drive Canadian society for decades until French Canada wins its freedom by default."

"No young man, you don't get it. English Canada will wait you out. You already have your freedom. Why don't you do something with it for God's sake?" The conversation was left dangling and Grierson returned to Scotland.

∞

Two years later, the NFB invited the indomitable Scotsman back. "We want your opinion about establishing a Film Training Centre at the NFB," said acting commissioner Grant McLean. "We need light to end the darkness, a way to discover new talent, and to relaunch the documentary. Expo 67 has led us to over hire. The filmmakers in the cafeteria are idle. If I fire them, there will be a nasty public uproar. What should I do?"

Grierson's response was immediate. "Use production monies to hire teachers, reward the best talent, and make *them* the creative core of a rejuvenated organization," he urged. "Let me light a fire under their too comfortable fannies."

He decided to address the production personnel on the newly constructed sound stage, a space that hundreds could fill easily. To ensure good attendance, an hour before he began, the Scots showman marched through the Film Board halls, young employees on either side of him. He raved at the top of his voice, "I'd fire the lot of them and start over again!" The staff was terrified by his presence.

The NFB cafeteria was full from morning to night. There was no money for production, so filmmakers sat and drank coffee. An hour later, the cafeteria emptied and the sound stage was full. "Most of you here know my philosophy. The NFB is primarily a national information service and it is as such that it has most to teach," he began.

He was furious with those filmmakers who insisted upon total freedom of expression. "It is a dangerous tendency to claim to be an artist and to be financed by the state *ad infinitum*, since one good school of art after another has been wiped out through such arrangements. Some of the very nicest films can be naïve not to say ignorant, amateurish, and even illiterate," was his incisive opinion.

"Some films can be professional yet still destructive for being politically hot." Most knew he was referring to the documentary *Bethune*, with its positive spin on a deceased, nonconformist, Canadian communist doctor, then circulating in (communist) Eastern Europe. "If there is one thing I know, it is that a footloose attitude to communism can destroy careers and organizations." Most everyone knew that the Department of External Affairs was outraged over this film for contradicting current (anti-communist) foreign policy. Thinking of the damage it was doing, Grierson closed his remarks with a final recommendation, "The NFB should rethink its relationship with government."

This was useful advice, but Ottawa had already chosen the prudent fiscal course of universal financial cutbacks. Grierson had tried to teach using low-key light. The results were discouraging. Some thought the agency was doomed. He wondered if the NFB would fade to black.

In 1967 the NFB used *cinéma vérité* in a series called
"Challenge for Change/Société Nouvelle." Grierson
worried that *Nell and Fred* and *The Things
I Cannot Change* might let an unsophisticated
person bring harm or ridicule to himself.

11

Passing the Torch

The sixty-nine-year-old returned to Scotland and kept an exhausting schedule of public appearances, film festival judging, and constant correspondence. In the fall of 1967 he collapsed and was hospitalized. His brother Anthony, a stern doctor, gave him the bad news: he had diseased lungs. "Your body must pay the dues for smoking and drinking excessively over a lifetime. If you do not stop, you will be dead in a year."

"But," Grierson protested, "I need the stuff to concentrate with."

"There is no bargaining with the Reaper," Anthony replied. "Quit or die." Grierson returned to

Wiltshire, where it took six months of Herculean strength, but he managed to break his daily habit of three packs of cigarettes and a bottle of alcohol. He confided to Margaret, "I am grateful for the extra innings." She too was ill, and her crippled hip made walking increasingly difficult. A year later, as usual, luck smiled. McGill University in Montreal offered him a professor's podium. Margaret insisted that he leave her behind. Reluctantly, he agreed.

It was mid-winter and McGill, located on five square blocks in downtown Montreal, was as bleak as the bare trees that filled it. On Grierson's first day, a taxi brought him from his hotel apartment to the steps of the central building in mid-campus. As he exited into a freezing rain, there was the tombstone of founder James McGill. He stopped to read the simple inscription, name, and dates. He muttered, "Another Scotsman. You won't be seeing me soon, Jimmy lad, I've got work to do here. One thing we both know. Education is the most important mass medium. You gave them books a hundred years ago. I am here to show the transformation of the motion picture into an instrument of educational policy. There will be no 'Rest in Peace' in my classes."

He entered a huge lecture hall in the building named after Stephen Leacock. The hall was packed with 350 hopeful filmmakers. Grierson sensed many students assumed the pleasure of being lost in a crowd. To combat this, he cleverly started his lecture by bellowing a stern admonition to a hyper-cool, bearded, sun-glassed student in a far corner. He had hoisted his boots on the seat ahead of him, "Get your feet off of that chair," Grierson began. "Where do you think you are, in your mother's living room? You may not respect the faculty, but you could at least show some respect for this institution." The red-faced radical collapsed into himself.

Grierson explained their first assignment: "Write a letter, 'Dear Mother' or 'Dear Father' and discuss an idea, any idea, about film. Then attach a passport-size photo of yourself so I know who is speaking." If he was breaking the formal rules of essay scholarship, he was also not allowing anyone to hide in the anonymous hundreds.

They listened intently. "What really counts is reading philosophy, literature, and history," he continued. Then he shocked them. "Mass media exploration should occur in relationship to disciplines like politics, anthropology, sociology, and aesthetics. A general bachelor's degree is far more valuable than one in film studies. The all around personality is far more useful to society than the so-called film specialist. Learning the nuts and bolts of filmmaking should come later." The wannabe directors were crushed.

This was an era of confrontation, of youth versus authority, and McGill was not spared the rhetoric and activism going on in the rest of North America. Two months later, Grierson, the old left-leaning progressive, would have no truck with so-called "political action," as student activists were then occupying the Administration building. "You think you are revolutionaries," he began one day, "You know nothing about revolution. If you hate being called children, sit down and do your homework. Get your facts right and then be tough minded. And if you are *really* serious, get control of the Coke concession on campus."

This advice stunned many, who realized two things: first, their basic education had robbed them of knowledge of the classics, and second, the profits from their consuming habits were going to business, not to themselves. This feisty, energetic, and sandy/silver-haired Scotsman might be old, but he was Right On.

Full of new energy on his pulpit, the sermonizing prophet enjoyed repeating the same broad principles that had motivated him over a lifetime. He bemoaned the general lack of intellectual rigour, and he berated his students for engaging in the equivalent of a children's crusade, with no relationship to the workers. "How you can make progress without a knowledge of human need, I don't know. Today's students know little of the past, of the classics." As he put it, "You can't talk about freedom without getting back to Plato and Kant. If you are going to discuss the individual artist in relation to the state you had better take account of Trotsky's *Literature and Revolution*, which will lead to Arnold's *Culture and Anarchy*. You kids are a politically naïve 'hollering generation' who have been bought off by parents and teachers. Neo-Trotskyites who haven't read Trotsky, anarchists who don't know that anarchists don't unite, and even fewer Leninists or Stalinists, for that means discipline."

He was fond of throwing students off balance, of first being authoritarian, then dismissive of their attempts to spell out positions, then encouraging them in a paternalistic way, especially the shy neophytes.

In his small seminars for upperclassmen, often meeting after hours in his hotel apartment, he would create caricatures from the group to emphasize pedagogical themes of politics or aesthetics. One student, whose name ended in "-sky", he turned into a resident Jewish intellectual. It made no difference the young man was a Polish Catholic. Another, whose dangling curly hair melded perfectly with his faded bluejeans (in an era when jeans were considered offensive), he called his "resident radical." When a female student claimed writer's block, he demolished her by insisting, "How dare you have the arrogance to label yourself 'writer'?"

The atmosphere was electric, as the master spared no one. If he seemed insensitive, it was his way of separating the timid from the talented. When he finally got around to discussing filmmaking at his seminars, not surprisingly, he denounced Film Board features and the contemporary fashion for the *auteur* principle, which put the director as the central creative force in a production. He also dismissed the North American rage for cheap, portable equipment like the 8mm camera. "Who gives a horse's rear for the 8mm revolution if it is going to let loose on us the 8mm mind? No, ladies and gentlemen, the most important mass medium of all is the medium of education. And to make sure we firm up the priorities that establish sentiments, loyalties, and powers of appreciation, the most important function of all is the teaching of teachers. I am looking for the creation of standards by which excellencies are measured."

Another time, a student's question about aesthetics reflected a changed Grierson. He described that giant of cinema, Sergei Eisenstein, as "the greatest master of public spectacle in the history of cinema. Yet, what the Russian filmmaker finally learned in his later years was how to be quiet." The lesson was clear: Film was as much art as propaganda.

∽

In these turbulent times, Grierson commented on the Film Board's experimental programme called "Challenge for Change/Société Nouvelle," which was providing citizens with access to film and video cameras to better communicate their needs and priorities. The initial idea came from Ottawa, which thought that the inarticulate impoverished people themselves might improve the democratic process, first by having professionals help them, then by making their own films or videos.

One of the first televised films was *The Things I Cannot Change*. It used direct cinema style to reveal a poverty-stricken Montreal family of nine children and unemployed parents caught in the teeth of grinding poverty. Over one million television viewers had watched. Grierson hated the film. "It reveals a family that is vulnerable and easy to exploit. They exposed their private lives and their neighbours mocked them for their candidness."

The whole process came under Grierson's scrutiny when Film Board veteran Colin Low shot a series of twenty-six short films on Newfoundland's Fogo Island.

He recorded the tension between the island's population and the provincial authorities who wanted to reset-
tle them. Low did not want to show the adversarial
relationship, but to allow images to explain the tension,
then the co-operation, that helped reshape the government's resettlement plan. He served as a mediator,
using his filmmaker's tools to find a point of common
interest. With a professional social worker, he showed
the edited material and led discussions around the
island for a month. Then he filmed some academics
discussing the material, and finally showed the
islanders a film made by the ministry of fisheries. In all,
he concluded a "communication loop" that enabled a
catalytic community process to occur. The islanders
stayed to form a fishing co-op, unemployment fell, and
fishermen earned good money. Best of all, this
approach reflected an interesting thoughtful humility
that allowed adversaries to meet halfway.

Grierson raised an important question about the
process when he invited Low to McGill. Few knew
Grierson had already turned 180 degrees and now
favoured citizens using media tools. He saw the effect:
the democratic process was strengthening. But he
wanted to provoke Low and the students and to make
clear the tension of economic versus social pressures.

"Low's presentation of local concerns is not necessarily the real representation of local concerns, much
less participatory democracy," he began by baiting the
audience. "There is something missing: the broad perspective worthy of a great country like Canada."

He cut off Low's protest in mid-sentence.
"Filmmakers tend to rush to the support of protesting

minorities," he continued. "Do you remember that Challenge for Change film we viewed that dealt with the closing down of an Alberta coal town? Canada is a sea of wide and difficult land spaces where boom towns are like islands of habitation that often go bust and become ghost towns after the wealth is extracted. There are countless distress centres elsewhere that merit attention. Why *should* a town continue after all its resources have been mined? There should be a sense of responsibility to the majority, established or even constitutional viewpoints."

He was not done roasting his guest. "You know, this whole programme lacks the broad perspective worthy of a great country – It is not 'news in depth.' You focus on subjects like the perplexities and sufferings of this rich Canadian people… Fat boys feeling sorry for themselves is a bad joke," he mocked. "The rest of the world will laugh at the absurdity of a rich country engaged in this kind of activity." The fierce Scotsman was blasting one of the great talents of Canadian documentary film. His students were perplexed.

This blunt technique did not fool Low, who understood the game. He was ready with a response, which echoed Grierson's earliest approach to film. "I am looking for human response in the quiet light of ordinary humanism," Low began. "To capture a moment of anger or ferocity might grab the viewer and be visually attractive, but it then sets in stone for all time an emotional state that may not in fact reflect the daily reality. We must not use the camera to exploit a moment, but to explore an atmosphere and to facilitate dialogue." Grierson could not have agreed with him more.

Low then went on to explain how his short films had reflected the dynamics of the human factors as opposed to economic factors. He concluded his defence by stating, "We must always be aware of the dangerous possibilities of exploitation of a subject. Our duty is exploration." The Fogo Island series became a major force in defining contemporary Canadian documentary film. When Low had finished, the students at last understood the tactic that Professor Grierson had been employing to teach them.

Out of the other side of his mouth, a few weeks later, Grierson praised a Challenge for Change documentary, *Nell and Fred*. An elderly couple, a landlady and her rooming tenant, considered the pros and cons of going into an institution. In the film's surprise ending, they decided to stay put. Grierson loved it for both revealing local life and proclaiming a universal message. "This film is a complete Chekovian experience," he enthused. "It captures the dramatic implications of changes in our own day. Why? Because it goes beyond reporting local problems and an objective discussion of local destinies." He loved its emotional centre of epic quality. "Unlike other films of this genre," he continued, "It does not teach chaos to a new generation that is hoping for order and a coherent future."

On this he was unwavering as he told his McGill students, "Anyone who tries to give anything else but the hope of a coherent future, cut his throat and hang him to the nearest lamppost." His recipe for success was, "Avoid embracing the world in promiscuous hand-fuls. Instead, drink with the people in the right places, listen to their conversations, ask the right questions, and get the right answers. Films should all revolve around Canada in the making."

By the fall of 1970, the campus was abuzz with talk about this Scots fireball who was electrifying classes. He returned often to his favourite analogy, see-ing Canada as a small, modest light that could be manipulated in the same way a lighthouse used a sys-tem of magnifying lenses to flash brilliantly around the vast horizon. "The goal of a communicator is to know either how to serve other people or how they wish to be served," he insisted. "There is no need to see gov-ernment or institutions as the Enemy. The Enemy is the gloom, alarm, and despondency of teachers and talkers. If artists abandoned their complacency and egotism and accentuated the positive, there would be many freedoms to discover."

As invigorating as teaching was, Grierson found it took much vital energy. Even though a number of graduate assistants were helping him handle the moun-tain of paper that teaching requires, the wear and tear was exhausting. He became ill a number of times and doctors ordered him to stay in bed. Students applauded when he returned, walking slower than before, with his familiar grey suit coat covering his cardigan sweater and tie.

Applause died and silence followed. He surveyed the sea of faces before him, and then dived into the adversarial method of teaching that allowed him to practise a familiar intellectual about-face. "I want to

provoke you to think and read before you repeat plati-
tudes about popular communication," he offered. "For
example, the fashion is to mouth the clichés of
Marshall McLuhan. He is a terrible writer."

"Do you mean to say that McLuhan is nonsense?"
asked one brave soul.

"Listen to what I said," he replied. "I said he
couldn't write. But even if he is hiring himself out to
big business for $10,000 a session, he understands the
new media tools are part of a healthy, if sometimes-
awkward process of renewing democracy. Look at how
progressive filmmakers are helping people to communicate with government and vice versa. They are teaching the public to take charge of their own destinies,
and to reach for social equality. That is McLuhan's
message to the massaged masses of the Mass Age."

"And watch out for glib apologists who pretend to
be medicine men," he warned. "The idea," he concluded, "is to discover universals that can be felt as
much as thought about. Never forget the importance of
local communities, and be aware that most mass
media, oriented towards consumerism, are undermin-
ing such communities. You must decentralize the
power of propaganda."

∞

One bright student remembered years later how
Grierson seemed to resemble the Everyman of the
twentieth century, a curious combination of a man who
had respect for certain conformities, yet was attached
to the irreconcilable. As he summed it up, "He was a

propagandist for ideas while also a peculiar amalgam of irreconcilable opposites. He swore like a drill sergeant, yet he quoted moral philosophers of whom most people had never heard. He loved democracy, yet referred to communist Russia as a place where planning and acting for the public good had transformed a nation. He called himself a propagandist, yet believed in acting on behalf of the common people and democracy within the existing system. His lectern was a pulpit."

The McGill years underscored how much Grierson thrived as a teacher. Five hundred people showed up at the student union to a party honouring him. A spotlight shone on him, but overcome with emotion, he said, "Please bring the house lights up. I would rather greet each of you personally." He spent the evening seated, a graduate student on each side of him, shaking hands with well-wishers. In his heart, this grandson of a lighthouse keeper felt he had done his best. Over a lifetime, he had used his own brilliance to teach about light. He had taught elite groups of torch-bearers to act on behalf of the people, not of corporations. Grierson taught them that the light of public duty was their first responsibility. As this moviemaker's life was moving toward a final "fade to black," he was pleased to see how many had caught the inspiration and idealism that he had kept through a lifetime. A few naysayers were peeved by his patriarchal authoritarianism. He did not care, for they had missed the point.

∞

In the spring of 1971 Grierson embarked on what became his last journey, a joint federal government/ NFB advisory mission to India to investigate how Canada could assist that nation's family planning programme. Arriving in New Delhi, he saw cows meandering through streets so tightly packed with cars and people it was a wonder that anyone or anything could move. The smell of cow dung and auto exhaust made him realize this was the strangest assignment he had ever undertaken: to recommend how film or print or both should be used to publicize birth control methods to India's half-billion-plus population.

Privately he scoffed, "Of all things, I have come to India in the name of family planning. It seems surrealist."

Undaunted, after several months' investigation, he had become accustomed to the sight of women's brilliant saris and men's white Nehru outfits, of westernized professionals who seemed above it all, of holy men straight out of the fourteenth century who pretended nothing was real but their chanting, and of untouchables, a group of wretched humanity whose gross poverty was unspeakable. The din of horns, the screech of brakes, and the shouts of unintelligible languages left him wondering if this really was the world's largest democracy or a place on the edge of chaos.

At last, he met with India's prime minister, Indira Gandhi, whose father, Jawaharlal Nehru, had brought this subcontinent into the contemporary world. The regal, wily politician caught him off guard when she said, "So this is the terrible John Grierson I have heard so much about. My advisers tell me to watch out, because you are always ready to start a sermon about documentary or propaganda. Are you going to lecture me then?"

"No, Madame Prime Minister," he smiled in his most engaging diplomatic way. "I have always believed that a prime minister holds a special place in a democracy. She or he is the only prime minister you've got, so you must approach the P.M. as her loyal servant."

Gandhi was disarmed immediately. He continued, "There is, nonetheless, Madame, an approach to birth control that has some relationship to a method of communication that the National Film Board of Canada has developed. The top-down mode of communication through television and film just won't work here, because four-fifths of the population is located in rural India outside the contemporary communications loop. The best approach is to use decentralized communication techniques. Place information materials in local centres. Produce them in the form of filmstrips, slides, and audiotapes, all involving local persons," he continued. "Local women could speak directly to female groups and respected local men could address the male population."

The prime minister looked over at her aide, "Listen to this prophet. He understands India."

∽

Back in England months later, Grierson was preparing to return to India. He noticed he was tiring easily and, hating to admit he might be ill, reported to the hospital at Bath for a checkup. The diagnosis was cancer of the liver and lung. Doctors told him he would be dead in a month.

Instead of yielding to depression and the inevitable, his mental state became even more acute. He filled the hospital room with newspapers, books, radio, tape recorder and television, with an indoor antenna strung across the room, making the whole scene look like a flimsy science fiction movie set. He spent his days dictating farewell letters. "This hospital sure thinks it has got me," he wrote. "I'll show them..." But he knew this battle was his last, and he allowed no visitors except for Margaret. He left strict orders to follow: cremation, no service, and burial at sea on a fishing boat off his favourite lighthouse point.

Two days before his death, Margaret asked, "John, what would you do if you had life to live over again?" Uncharacteristically silent for a moment, he then spoke, "The spice of life is its pitfalls. But there's never been a pitfall that the human spirit can't dig itself out of. The most dangerous pitfall is the loss of faith in the human spirit. If that happens, remember – it's you that's at fault." Perhaps this was meant to be his epitaph. On February 19, 1972, the nurse found him with a microphone in his hand, a tape recorder reel spinning aimlessly, its tape having run out.

In 1971, India asked Grierson how they might address family planning. He concluded that the best approach was not film, but to decentralize information systems. Before he could conclude his report, illness struck and his life ended.

Epilogue

The Grierson Legacy

There have been a number of authors in the last decade who have dismissed Grierson for his pie-in-the-sky theory of documentary, that public information and persuasion, i.e., propaganda, could make better citizens and a better country. Others think that feature film is the best way to speak to citizens and the rest of the world about a nation's culture. Their resistance to Grierson's documentary approach is based on a conviction that public monies are best spent on promoting feature entertainment.

Since 1964, the Canadian government has spent billions of dollars underwriting features and television fare. English Canada has produced largely B-features that few Canadians and even fewer non-Canadians have seen. The Quebec feature film has fared better because inherent in its films, even in the shallowest and most profitable, *Les Boys* and *Elvis Gratton*, is the expression of a language and culture to which the Québécois must remain loyal. Several English Canadian directors like David Cronenberg and Atom Egoyan are now world renowned, but one could argue that they would have achieved success with or without government funding.

On the plus side, the millions spent on forgettable features and television fare have provided employment to technicians and built a film industry infrastructure and billion-dollar-a-year industry. This is good, economically speaking. Yet the U.S. domination of distribution remains, as it has since the beginning, a fixed reality that translates into less than 3 percent of the annual theatrical audience for Canadian productions in the present and foreseeable future. A weak Canadian dollar guaranteed the cheap overhead that attracted many U.S. producers to shoot in Canadian locales. Their features and television shows pretended to be American and as a whole, did little for Canadian culture, citizens, or the national reality. The public treats Canadian television fare (other than sports) as mostly forgettable time fillers. Grierson was not wrong to thumb his nose at this no-win situation and to insist on a continuing National Film Board to do the honest work that needed to be done.

He remained wedded to the idea that the documentary serves as an effective means to achieve citizenship education. This was at the core of his contribution to Canada. From the 1930s, Grierson insisted that not only could average citizens be affected by exposure to the mass medium of film, but so too could the opinion leaders/educators who help harness mass energies. If Grierson was wrong, it was in his belief that corporate energies would unite with technocrats to bring order to contemporary society.

Corporate energies are devoted principally to profit, not to the prophet, and Grierson should not be faulted for his inability to turn corporate institutions into instruments that help the masses make sense of contemporary life. Canada, in the crisis of war, showed how well collective effort could work; in peacetime, there were few who wished for heroic national effort. In fact, once a national crisis passes, the brave new world that is promised is often hollow in practice. People tend to ask that they be left alone as a reward for their sacrifice. Grierson thought this was wrong. He wanted the state to use its energies and wealth to help make life better for all.

To sum up this fiery propagandist, we think of Grierson's documentary legacy to Canada: when he described documentary as the creative interpretation of actuality, he meant the management of collective attitudes by manipulating significant symbols. Film images were not to be understood as literal reflections of the world, but as ways to evoke other symbolic meanings, much as poetry works in language. At McGill, he often insisted, "Everything is beautiful – if you get it in the right order." He believed that the French word *imaginer* was what propaganda should do, but there is no exact English translation (to imagine, conceive, devise are not sufficient) that captures the full nuance of how *imaginer* was to serve as a kind of trigger to propel people.

It is doubtful that Grierson would have approved of today's "point of view" documentary, because too often it smacks of uninspired themes, "peeping Tomism," and tends to lack hope. He had no problem with an elite functioning as propagandists or educators if they reflected democratic ideas, not those of the politically powerful or of big business. Grierson's definition conflicts with a popular contemporary definition of propaganda that appears to remain neutral, valueless, and circular. Today's definition is, "the deliberate and systematic attempt to shape perceptions, manipulate cognitions, and direct behaviour to achieve a response that furthers the desired attempt of the propagandist."

Grierson thought the propagandist/documentarist should proclaim fearlessly that the object was public or universal values and well being, not individual gain on behalf of the dominant classes or the dominant ideology. His understanding from the beginning was that propaganda was education, a public duty to help liberate the confused, the uninformed, and the lost. John Grierson was a trailblazer who shaped Canadian documentary film. He devoted his life to documentary as "the eyes of democracy." His life celebrated every possibility to improve humanity in a world of ragged human endeavour.

"The honest work that still needs to be done can be done
by the documentary, which serves as an effective means
to achieve citizenship education."

Chronology of John Grierson (1898-1972)

Compiled by Gary Evans

JOHN GRIERSON AND HIS TIMES

CANADA AND THE WORLD

1891
American William Dickson, working in Thomas A. Edison's research laboratory since 1889, invents the first motion picture camera, the Kinetograph, and a peephole viewer, the Kinetoscope.

1894
The earliest complete film on record (Library of Congress, Washington, D.C.), an *Edison Kinetoscope Record of a Sneeze*, is an "actuality" (a real event) later referred to as *Fred Ott's Sneeze*.

1895
In France, brothers Louis and Auguste Lumière invent the *Cinématographe* and begin making the first motion pictures. They present

John Grierson

John Grierson and His Times

Canada and the World

ten short films (*actualités*) on March 22 in France, including *The Arrival of a Train at La Ciotat*. Audiences are thrilled by cinema's documentary realism. Movies soon become popular entertainment for rich and poor alike.

1896
On June 28, movies appear in Montreal; Edison films appear in July in Ottawa. Movies are called "White Magic."

1897
The British Empire celebrates Queen Victoria's Golden Jubilee.

1898
John Grierson is born in Deanston, Scotland, the fourth child of two schoolteachers who will have eight children.

1898
To attract immigrants, the CPR hires James Freer to tour Britain with his actuality films of western Canada.

1900
Actuality films record Canadian troop departures to fight the Boer War in South Africa.

1901
Queen Victoria dies and is succeeded by her son, King Edward VII.

1902
The Boer War ends.

The CPR engages Briton Charles Urban to lure prospective immigrants to Canada with his "scenics" of Canadian landscapes.

JOHN GRIERSON AND HIS TIMES

CANADA AND THE WORLD

In France, Georges Méliès makes *Le Voyage dans la lune* (*A Trip to the Moon*), one of the first attempts to use film as a narrative and also the first science fiction film. He invents special effects.

1903
Grierson's mother Jane runs a soup kitchen for the poor. His mother's idealism encourages him to develop a lifelong sense of social responsibility.

1903
American film director Edwin S. Porter makes *The Great Train Robbery*. Porter's chase sequence becomes a model for future Canadian and U.S. (fiction) films.

1904
Grierson sees his first movies in school. They are actualities of Canadian landscapes. The images spark a lifelong attraction to Canada and nonfiction film.

1904
Work begins on the Panama Canal. Nickelodeons (permanent "nickel theatres") begin appearing across North America.

1905
Alberta and Saskatchewan become provinces of Canada.

1907
Moviemakers begin moving from the eastern U.S. to Hollywood, where better year-round light conditions will allow for an increased number of productions. Nickelodeons attract one million patrons per day.

1908
Grierson excels at school and his teachers claim that he achieves "effortless superiority."

1908
American companies shoot melodramatic Canadian stories both in Canada and the U.S. American control of filmmaking and distribution hinders development of an indigenous Canadian film industry.

John Grierson

JOHN GRIERSON AND HIS TIMES	CANADA AND THE WORLD

1912
The S.S. *Titanic* sinks.

1913
Hollywood makes 60 percent of U.S. movies and is known as the moviemaking capital. Audiences embrace the feature or headline film (forty-fifty minutes of lavish images).

The National Gallery of Canada is incorporated.

1914
The First World War begins. Canada is automatically at war alongside Britain.

Canada's first newsreel, *Canadian Animated Weekly*, features troops training and mock battles; cinematographers were not allowed to film war footage. Across Canada, men rush to enlist.

In the U.S, 3000-seat "dream palaces" appear.

1915
Grierson, just 17, graduates from high school and joins the Royal Navy. He spends the next four years as a telegraphist on minesweepers in the North Sea.

1915
British born Charlie Chaplin becomes internationally famous with his satirical Hollywood comedies pitting a poor tramp against a heartless system.

American D.W. Griffith will become the master of film techniques with his landmark *The Birth of a Nation*.

JOHN GRIERSON AND HIS TIMES

1916
Grierson spends his off hours on ship studying and learning university level material.

1918
Seeing men killed in war at sea convinces Grierson that after the war he must do something with his life to make issues of peace more exciting than war itself.

1919
Grierson begins studies at the University of Glasgow, where he is in a rebellious mood after the war years.

1920
Grierson writes poetry and film reviews for the university literary magazine. Charlie Chaplin, representing "the little man," is his favourite star.

CANADA AND THE WORLD

1916
Canadian newsreel propaganda produced in Britain encourages enlistment and patriotism in Canada.

1917
In Russia, the Bolshevik Party seizes power in the October Revolution.

In Canada, artist Tom Thomson drowns in Algonquin Park.

1918
The formation of the Exhibits and Publicity Bureau to promote trade and commerce will establish Canada as the world's longest-enduring government-sponsored filmmaker of travelogues and nonfiction films.

In November, the First World War ends. Of the 37 million casualties, 60,000 are Canadian dead.

1919
The Winnipeg General Strike alarms Canadian politicians, many of whom see ties between organized labour and Russia's communist revolution.

1920
The CPR buys half interest in Associated Screen News (ASN). ASN makes newsreels in Canada that will circulate at home and abroad for the next two decades,

Grierson's sympathies are with the Clydeside labour movement, which forms in response to widespread unemployment and poverty in the U.K.

serving as major advertisements for tourism.

Canada joins the League of Nations.

1921

W.L. Mackenzie King begins his first term as prime minister of Canada. He will become the longest serving Canadian prime minister.

The Communist Party of Canada is formed in Guelph, Ontario.

Hollywood emerges as the most powerful producer of films in the world.

1922

Sermonizing at Highland churches, Grierson states that faith in oneself, hard thinking, and actively struggling for good are essential human activities.

1922

The documentary feature *Nanook of the North*, shot on Hudson Bay by the American Robert Flaherty, puts Canada as a subject on the map of world cinema.

In Britain, unemployed Glasgow workers undertake a hunger March on London.

The Union of Soviet Socialist Republics (U.S.S.R.) is formed from the former Russian empire.

In the U.S.S.R., Lev Kuleshov experiments with montage, (editing). Montage makes films more emotionally engaging.

1923

Grierson completes his Master of Arts degree. He begins teaching

1923

Ottawa changes the name Exhibits and Publicity Bureau to the

JOHN GRIERSON AND HIS TIMES

school in the slums of Newcastle upon Tyne, England.

CANADA AND THE WORLD

Canadian Government Motion Picture Bureau. The Bureau continues making newsreels and travelogues until 1941.

Paramount Pictures of Hollywood wins control of most first-run cinemas in Canada through Famous Players Canadian Corporation.

1924

Grierson is awarded a Rockefeller Foundation fellowship to study at the University of Chicago. There he begins studying the mass media, especially newspapers and film.

1924

The Labour Party under Ramsay MacDonald forms the first left-wing government in Britain.

1925

Grierson moves to New York, where he meets famed editor Walter Lippmann, who inspires him to turn to film as an educational tool. He also meets documentary filmmaker Robert Flaherty.

Grierson travels to major American cities, then returns to Chicago to write a newspaper column on art.

1925

In the U.S.S.R, Sergei Eisenstein makes *Battleship Potemkin*, a film celebrating the twentieth anniversary of a failed revolution that anticipated the later Bolshevik victory. In spite of heavy censorship outside the U.S.S.R., the film's use of montage is recognized worldwide for being artistic and avant-garde.

1926

Grierson introduces the word "documentary" into film language while reviewing Robert Flaherty's film, *Moana*.

1926

In London, the Empire Marketing Board (EMB) is formed to use publicity, including film, to increase trade throughout the British Empire.

1927

Returning to Britain, Grierson begins working at the EMB, specializing in film publicity.

1927

Sound film arrives from Hollywood. *The Jazz Singer*, starring Al Jolson, heralds the end the silent film era.

John Grierson

John Grierson and His Times	Canada and the World
1928 Grierson begins working as director, editor, and writer of *Drifters*, his own documentary on herring fishing. Margaret Taylor joins him as assistant editor. *Drifters* will become Grierson's hallmark as he turns to producing rather than directing films for the next three decades.	**1928** Canada's most expensive feature film fiasco, the First World War melodrama *Carry On, Sergeant!*, fails because of lack of U.S. distribution.
1929 In Britain, *Drifters* is shown with *Battleship Potemkin* in London and receives instant acclaim. Grierson engages eighteen filmmakers and forms the nucleus of the documentary film movement.	**1929** In October, the stock market crashes, sending economic shock waves around the world and touching off the Great Depression.
1930 John Grierson and Margaret Taylor are secretly married.	**1930** Drought on the Prairies signals a coming decade of crop failure and collapse of the wheat economy. Canada's first sound feature, *The Viking*, directed by American Varrick Frissell, captures footage of the ice floes off Newfoundland. Frissell and twenty-five crew members die while shooting supplementary footage of the annual seal hunt.
1931 The EMB sends Grierson to Ottawa, Canada, where he studies the organization of the Canadian Government Motion Picture Bureau and all things Canadian.	**1931** The Statute of Westminster creates the idea of the Commonwealth to replace Empire. It recognizes the autonomy of Britain, Canada, South Africa, Australia, New Zealand, and the Irish Free State. Canada may now make its own foreign policy.

John Grierson and His Times

1932
Robert Flaherty joins the EMB documentary unit. Flaherty's time with the unit gives birth to *Industrial Britain*, a documentary classic.

1933
The EMB closes, a victim of the Depression. Grierson's documentary film unit finds a new home at the General Post Office (GPO) in Britain and flourishes. Of the EMB films Grierson states, "they were films of ordinary people and the dignities of life in our time."

1934
Alberto Cavalcanti, famous for his work with sound, joins the GPO unit and encourages the idea of narrative documentary style.

Canada and the World

1932
Franklin Roosevelt is elected president of the U.S.; he will be re-elected three more times, 1936, 1940, and 1944.

The Ottawa Conference makes it clear that each member of the Commonwealth must stand alone in weathering the Great Depression.

Associated Screen News of Montreal, renowned for its ten-minute theatrical shorts, produces *Canadian Cameos*.

1933
Canada's gross national product has declined by 42 percent since the beginning of the Depression; 30 percent of the work force is unemployed.

Hitler comes to power in Germany. He is known to watch movies every night in his own private theatre, a practice he will continue until his death.

1934
Since 1929, Conservative Prime Minister R.B. Bennett has done little to help Canadians through the Depression.

The Canadian Government Motion Picture Bureau loses funding and subsequently international markets.

John Grierson

JOHN GRIERSON AND HIS TIMES

CANADA AND THE WORLD

1935

Grierson gives his blessing to a new realistic approach to documentary. *Housing Problems*, directed by Edgar Anstey and Ruby Grierson (John's sister), is one of the first examples of what would much later be called "direct cinema" or *cinéma vérité*.

1935

Liberal William Lyon Mackenzie King defeats R.B. Bennett to become prime minister. Two new parties, the CCF and Social Credit, appear in Parliament.

Many people hide from the realities of the Depression in Canada and the U.S. by going to the movies. Alfred Hitchcock becomes internationally renowned as a director of mystery thrillers.

1936

Grierson is executive producer of *Night Mail*, directed by Harry Watt. W.H Auden and Benjamin Britten are responsible for its poetry and music.

Ross McLean, from the office of Canada's High Commissioner to London, recommends Grierson be sent to Canada to help the ailing Motion Picture Bureau.

1936

Mussolini and Hitler create the Rome-Berlin Axis.

Hollywood studios (MGM, Paramount, Warner Brothers, 20th Century Fox, and RKO) reach their zenith. The major directors of the studio era are Josef Von Sternberg, John Ford, Howard Hawks, and Alfred Hitchcock. Colour film comes to Hollywood.

1937

Prime Minister King meets Hitler and warns him that Canada will stand with Britain if another war comes.

1938

Grierson sails to Canada, where he meets Prime Minister King and advises the government how best to use mass media to bring Canada alive to its citizens. He recommends centralizing government film activities in a new body.

1938

Hitler marches into Austria; Britain tries to appease Germany at Munich.

King closes Canada's doors to refugees trying to flee Hitler.

JOHN GRIERSON AND HIS TIMES

1939

The outbreak of war in September gives the NFB its rationale for the next six years – producing propaganda to unite the country.

Grierson becomes Government Film Commissioner and stays at his post until August 1945. He defines propaganda as *education* and sees the war as a vehicle to make a more democratic society.

1940

Grierson brings in experts from abroad to train young Canadian recruits fresh from university. He hires many women to carry out the war work.

Grierson produces films to improve Mackenzie King's poor public image.

The NFB's monthly theatrical newsreel series, *Canada Carries On*, begins circulating in 800 Canadian cinemas. There are French versions that help bring information on world events to French Canada.

1941

The NFB absorbs the Motion Picture Bureau. Grierson orders completion of a national distribution

CANADA AND THE WORLD

1939

On May 2, the National Film Board is created.

The Second World War begins on September 1 with Germany's invasion of Poland. Canada declares war on Germany on September 7.

Hollywood's opulent "blockbusters" *Gone With the Wind* and *The Wizard of Oz* allow audiences to escape into romantic melodrama and fantasy. The former becomes the largest grossing film of all time until *Star Wars* (1977).

1940

Prime Minister King hopes to avoid conscription and national division through volunteerism.

Prime Minister Winston Churchill's wartime speeches in Britain stir millions while Mackenzie King's seem lifeless.

In the U.S., Orson Welles makes *Citizen Kane*, a poorly disguised attack on newspaper mogul William Randolph Hearst. The film fails for lack of publicity in the powerful Hearst press, but in the mid-1950s after Hearst's death it will be acclaimed as one of the greatest films of all time.

1941

On December 7, Japan bombs Pearl Harbor; the U.S., Canada, and Britain declare war on Japan.

JOHN GRIERSON AND HIS TIMES

circuit to cover Canadian non-theatrical film. NFB films circulate in hundreds of schools and libraries.

1942

Canada wins its first ever Academy Award for *Churchill's Island*, a 1941 theatrical newsreel proclaiming Britain's fearlessness in the face of German aerial attacks. A second NFB theatrical series, *The World in Action*, reaches millions internationally with screen editorials that explain the patterns of a world at war.

Grierson works himself to exhaustion and recuperates in Florida, where he begins a manuscript, *The Eyes of Democracy*, a testament to his faith in propaganda. The book will not be published until 1990.

1943

Grierson agrees to head the Wartime Information Board for a year. The Board serves as a central co-ordinating agency for public information. Prime Minister King allows him to use polls, a new technique of measuring public opinion, but results are to be kept secret.

CANADA AND THE WORLD

Within days, Japan captures the Canadian garrison in Hong Kong; 557 Canadians are killed or die in prison camps.

1942

Hollywood documentaries like Frank Capra's *Why We Fight* series are useful tools to explain war aims.

In August, Canadian troops suffer heavy losses in the Dieppe Raid, which demonstrates faulty Allied planning. NFB propaganda tries to cushion the bad news with a promise. "We'll be back..."

1943

Canada experiences its worst year of strikes since 1919. Polls show the public approves of Ottawa's control of wartime prices and wages.

Prime Minister Mackenzie King holds a plebiscite, which frees him from his earlier "no conscription" pledge.

Hollywood, influenced by documentary methods, makes realistic and convincing combat films.

John Grierson and His Times

1944

Called "Propaganda Maestro" in the national press, Grierson is at the peak of his powers and national influence in Canada.

NFB propaganda, shown regularly in cinemas and schools, avoids contentious issues like conscription, Japanese-Canadian internment, and the Holocaust.

Knowing the impossibility of competing with Hollywood, Grierson opposes the creation of a Canadian feature film industry. Instead, he encourages the making of short films shot by Canadian talent as being more likely to be distributed.

1945

Grierson resigns from the NFB to start an international documentary production company in New York.

Soviet cipher clerk Igor Gouzenko defects in Ottawa, and his documents reveal the existence of an operating spy network. Grierson, unaware that his former secretary was linked to the scandal, comes under scrutiny by investigators. Prime Minister King turns his back on Grierson.

Canada and the World

1944

Allied forces invade Normandy, France on D-Day, June 6. Canadian casualties number 1,074 killed, wounded, and missing.

King introduces conscription, but few of the 20,000 conscripts will ever see action because the war will end.

1945

Canadian troops liberate western Holland.

U.S. President Roosevelt dies of cerebral hemorrhage and Harry Truman succeeds him in April.

Germany surrenders in May.

In Britain, Winston Churchill is defeated by Clement Attlee, whose Labour government stays in power until 1951.

In August, the U.S. drops two atomic bombs on Japan. On September 2, Japan surrenders. The Second World War ends.

JOHN GRIERSON AND HIS TIMES	CANADA AND THE WORLD
	Roberto Rossellini directs *Rome, Open City*, a melodrama using location shooting to describe Germany's occupation of Rome in 1943-44. His film style, called "neorealism," will influence world cinema for decades.

1946

Grierson is called to testify before the Royal Commission on Espionage in Government Service in Ottawa. The Federal Bureau of Investigation (FBI) in Washington, assuming guilt by association, prevents him from working in the U.S.

1946

The Cold War begins.

Former Prime Minister Churchill makes his "Iron Curtain" speech in the U.S. The hunt for communists reflects a national paranoia in the U.S. as fear of atomic warfare and the U.S.S.R. grows.

1947

Grierson joins UNESCO in Paris for a year as adviser with responsibility for mass media and public relations. He argues idealistically for a world that enjoys freedom of information.

1947

The Massey-Lévesque Royal Commission on the Arts leads to federal funding of the arts in Canada. This support, continuing to the present, helps build and sustain Canadian national culture.

In Washington, the House Committee on Un-American Activities begins a hunt for communists. The Hollywood Ten Blacklist is created.

1948

The Central Office of Information (C.O.I.) in London hires Grierson as controller of its film operations. Because of little ministerial support and less interest by Europe as a whole, he fails to revive the British documentary.

1948

An ailing Mackenzie King retires and is succeeded by Louis Saint-Laurent as prime minister of Canada.

In the U.S., the Supreme Court orders Hollywood studios to divest themselves of their exhibition cir-

JOHN GRIERSON AND HIS TIMES

CANADA AND THE WORLD

cuits. This loss fatally weakens the monolithic studio system.

Reflecting the impact of documentary film, studios turn to producing cheaper social consciousness films, often on location, and semi-documentary melodramas that point to social malaise and postwar disenchantment in the U.S.

1949

Ottawa censors the NFB film *The People Between* for being pro-communist in its recognition of the existence of the People's Republic of China.

1949

Canada is one of the founders of the North Atlantic Treaty Organization (NATO).

In China, Mao Zedong proclaims the People's Republic of China.

Reflecting postwar moral anxiety, Hollywood produces *film noir*, films that are criminal melodramas emphasizing greed, lust, cruelty, and human depravity.

1950

The National Film Board is accused of having communist employees. Ottawa installs a new film commissioner with no ties to the Grierson era.

1950

Under UN auspices, Canada sends forces to fight in the Korean war alongside the U.S.

In Washington, Senator Joseph McCarthy conducts a vendetta against alleged communists and their sympathizers. This period lasts until 1954. The use of unsubstantiated accusations to hound and investigate will henceforth be called *McCarthyism*.

JOHN GRIERSON AND HIS TIMES

1951
Grierson becomes executive producer at Group 3, an experimental British enterprise that tries to make story films in documentary style. The indifference of the commercial film industry seals its fate. Group 3 fails.

1952
Norman McLaren's live action animation, *Neighbours*, wins an Academy Award. *Neighbours* becomes the most viewed film worldwide in NFB history and underscores the excellence of Canadian animation technique.

1953
Tuberculosis is discovered in Grierson's lungs and he must convalesce in England for a year.

CANADA AND THE WORLD

1951
Ottawa intends to keep the NFB and makes plans to relocate the agency to new facilities in Montreal.

1952
King George VI dies and is succeeded by his daughter, Queen Elizabeth II.

The Canadian Broadcasting Corporation inaugurates broadcast television.

Hollywood's blacklisting of so-called subversives now extends to over three hundred persons who are unable to work in the industry.

Hollywood introduces audiences to Cinerama, a new three-camera/projector widescreen process with stereo sound. In addition, a new format called 3-D appears, a stereoscopic process that mimics three-dimensional human perception.

1953
In the U.S.S.R., Nikita Khrushchev succeeds Joseph Stalin.

The Cold War and McCarthyism in the U.S. continue unabated.

Hollywood introduces widescreen CinemaScope, which lasts until

JOHN GRIERSON AND HIS TIMES

CANADA AND THE WORLD

1960. Between 1953-1954 it produces sixty-nine 3-D films, in which audiences wearing special glasses can enjoy the illusory depth of "Natural Vision."

1954
As Group 3 closes in Britain, Grierson returns to Scotland. From here, he often journeys abroad to be a juror at international film festivals.

1954
The Free Cinema movement emerges in British features. Such films overthrow bourgeois traditions in favour of liberal working class values. Free Cinema will influence documentary film style in Canada.

1955
Hollywood uses new widescreen filmmaking practices to compete with television. Blockbusters of three hours and longer will follow.

1956
New National Film Board headquarters open in Montreal.

1956
Egypt's nationalization of the Suez Canal and support of terrorism against Israel provoke a joint British, French, and Israeli attack on Egypt.

Lester Pearson proposes to use United Nations forces to halt the war and enforce peace. Pearson wins the Nobel Peace Prize.

1957
Grierson visits the new Film Board in Montreal and submits a report to the NFB critical of its bureaucracy. He fails to convince the CBC to run more NFB films.

1957
The Canada Council for the Arts is founded.

In France, the first *nouvelle vague*, or "New Wave" films appear. New Wave encourages a director's stylistic signature.

John Grierson

JOHN GRIERSON AND HIS TIMES	CANADA AND THE WORLD

JOHN GRIERSON AND HIS TIMES

Grierson returns to Scotland to work on a television channel owned by Scots-Canadian newspaper tycoon Roy Thomson. He hosts *This Wonderful World*, a showcase for documentaries, for the next decade.

CANADA AND THE WORLD

1958
The NFB leads the world in the development of "direct cinema"/ *cinéma vérité*, an innovative documentary film style in which the camera captures a decisive (human) moment. New lightweight equipment makes this change possible.

1959
In France, three major films of the New Wave appear. This self-reflexive cinema, like the *cinéma vérité* style of documentary, draws attention to the process of film-making itself as an ideological process. New Wave also revitalizes British and American filmmaking during the 1960s.

1960
John F. Kennedy becomes president of the U.S.

In Quebec, following the death of Maurice Duplessis, the Quiet Revolution begins.

In the U.S., the coming decade will mark the absorption of most of Hollywood's established studios by conglomerates. Panavision replaces CinemaScope.

JOHN GRIERSON AND HIS TIMES

1961

In Britain, Grierson is appointed a Commander of the Order of the British Empire in recognition of his years of service to the Commonwealth.

1962

Grierson erases years of bad feelings toward the U.S. after he is invited to speak there. Later this year he joins the jury of the Vancouver Film Festival. He also receives the Royal Canadian Academy of Arts Medal in recognition of his contribution to the visual arts in Canada

1963

Besides hosting *This Wonderful World*, Grierson is a juror at overseas film festivals at Belgrade and Venice. He continues to advise the Films of Scotland Committee.

In Canada, tentative efforts at feature film production start at the NFB in English and French, but lack of funding limits possibilities.

1964

Invited to the NFB's twenty-fifth anniversary, Grierson strengthens his links with Canada and reminds its filmmakers they are public servants.

CANADA AND THE WORLD

1961

The United States enters the Vietnam War.

Britain's "New Cinema" of social realism will peak in 1963. It borrows from Italian neorealism, Free Cinema, and the New Wave. Many of its directors will move to Hollywood and later influence U.S. filmmaking profoundly.

1962

The Cuban Missile Crisis brings the U.S. and U.S.S.R. to the brink of war.

Hollywood is unable to compete with television. The movie audience falls dramatically and Hollywood's income is half its 1946 figure.

1963

Lester B. Pearson is elected prime minister of Canada. In November, President John F. Kennedy is assassinated in Dallas, Texas.

1964

Marshall McLuhan's *Understanding Media: The Extensions of Man* is published.

JOHN GRIERSON AND HIS TIMES	**CANADA AND THE WORLD**

<table>
<tr><td></td><td>After numerous financial disasters, Hollywood turns to distributing independent European "art films" influenced by French and Italian film styles. This signals the approaching end of the studio system and the end of cultural taboos related to sex and violence in film.</td></tr>
<tr><td></td><td>

1965
Canada adopts a national flag.</td></tr>
<tr><td>

1966
Grierson is asked back to Canada by the NFB for an analysis of its present and future. He advocates creating a film training center, reducing staff, and closer relations with Ottawa. His advice is ignored.</td><td>

1966
The NFB prepares for the Centennial. Overhiring will lead to the NFB's near economic ruin by the end of the decade.</td></tr>
<tr><td>

1967
Lifelong abuse of tobacco and alcohol lead to Grierson's physical collapse. He gives up both, recuperates, and extends his life.</td><td>

1967
Canada and Montreal host the World's Fair, Expo 67, in celebration of Canada's centenary.

Ottawa forms the Canadian Film Development Corporation (CFDC), a $10-million bank to underwrite the foundation of a feature film industry. The NFB is excluded from this new deal.

Hollywood's *Bonnie and Clyde* (Arthur Penn) heralds the new American cinema, echoing the anti-establishment thrust of the next generation.</td></tr>
<tr><td>

1968
Upon recovering his health, Grierson makes *I Remember, I*</td><td>

1968
Pierre Trudeau succeeds Lester Pearson as prime minister of</td></tr>
</table>

Remember, a biographical documentary of his life in documentary film.

Canada and promptly slashes federal departmental budgets across the board.

Stanley Kubrick's *2001: A Space Odyssey* becomes the emblem of the Space Age. Its special effects will influence future filmmaking profoundly.

1969
Grierson begins teaching at McGill University in Montreal and inspires another generation of students of the documentary film. He also advises the Canadian Radio and Television Commission on communications policy.

1969
Ottawa believes separatists exist in many federal organisms including the NFB and Radio-Canada. Quebec's independence movement threatens national unity.

1970
Grierson leaves McGill and accepts an NFB assignment to advise India on how to communicate public service messages to its hundreds of millions of citizens. He discusses the issue with Prime Minister Indira Ghandi.

1970
In Canada, Prime Minister Trudeau invokes the War Measures Act during the October Crisis in Quebec.

The Canadian widescreeen process, IMAX, is introduced at the World's Fair in Osaka, Japan. A 3 D effect will be added in 1995.

1971
Grierson's work is interrupted as he is diagnosed with cancer. He returns to his home in England.

1972
In February, Grierson dies in hospital in Bath, England. His last will forbids a funeral, and after cremation, his ashes are scattered at sea off Scotland. His contribution to

1972
By the end of the 1970s, fewer than half the 160 Hollywood features produced annually are major films. Their creative vitality is questionable.

JOHN GRIERSON AND HIS TIMES

Canadian (and world) documentary film is incalculable.

CANADA AND THE WORLD

Canadian tax incentives will lead to dozens of Canadian feature films produced by the end of this decade, yet only a few achieve international merit. In spite of this, Canadian documentaries and animations remain popular.

Acknowledgments

Over the thirty years I have been teaching and writing about Grierson and film, friends and colleagues have shared their insights and stories, some of which appear in this book. Their recollections and observations invariably come back to the man, his idealism and his importance to Canada. He touched us all deeply.

Adam Symansky and Ron Blumer, both award-winning and world-renowned documentarians today, sat in the McGill University Grierson seminars with me. In our infrequent meetings over the years, we have continued to speculate about the 'perfect' Grierson film. I offer this book as one such possible film.

At the National Film Board of Canada, there are past and present film artists who shared their recollections of Grierson and also helped with this project. Film Commissioner Jacques Bensimon generously encouraged this book, Laurie Jones at NFB Communications also helped tremendously, as has the staff at the NFB Photothèque, Sophie Quevillon and Claude Lord. NFB Archivist Bernard Lutz has been a true friend and colleague over the years. Tom Daly, Colin Low, Wolf Koenig, Bob Verrall, Roger Blais, Bill Weintraub, Don Brittain, Len Chatwin, Rita Kilpatrick and Marjorie McKay all shared their memories of Grierson too. In the U.K., filmmaker Laurence Henson and Professor Ian Lockerbie of the Grierson Archive, Stirling, Scotland have contributed to building the Grierson mythology along with Forsyth Hardy. A number of colleagues at the university level deserve mention for their encouragement: I appreciated the collegiality of professors Sherry Ferguson and Patrick Brunet at the University of Ottawa, and in particular Professor Robert Babe, whose chapter on Grierson in his book on Canadian media theory prompted me to examine another aspect of Grierson's importance to Canada. Professors Peter Ohlin and Marianne Stenbaek of McGill University, and Professor Jack C. Ellis of Northwestern University shared their thoughts, ideas, and insights over the years.

At XYZ, my biggest thank you goes to editor Rhonda Bailey, whose unfailing energy and optimism brought this project to fruition. Darcy Dunton's superb index covers all things perfectly. Noreen Banow offered some valuable insights. In Montreal, André Vanasse kept the XYZ ship on course during a difficult time for the industry. Editorial Board member Terry Rigelhof, along with Doug Rollins, also encouraged this project. They have been colleagues and close associates for over twenty-five years. And to Dr. Karin Doerr of Concordia University, the closest collaborator of all, I owe everlasting thanks, for being there, through gales and fair weather, always.

Sources Consulted

Aitken, Ian. *Film and Reform: John Grierson and the Documentary Film Movement*. London: Routledge, 1990.

Ellis, Jack C. *John Grierson: Life, Contributions, Influence*. Carbondale, IL: Southern Illinois University Press, 2000.

Evans, Gary. *John Grierson: The Politics of Wartime Propaganda, 1939-1945*. Toronto: University of Toronto Press, 1984.

Evans, Gary. *In the National Interest: A Chronicle of the National Film Board of Canada, 1949-89*. Toronto: University of Toronto Press, 1991.

Grierson, John. *The Eyes of Democracy*. Ian Lockerbie, ed. Stirling, Scotland: John Grierson Archive, University of Stirling, 1990.

Hardy, Forsyth. *John Grierson:A Documentary Biography*. London: Faber and Faber, 1979.

Historical Journal of Film, Radio and Television 9, no. 3 (1989) Special issue: "John Grierson: A Critical Retrospective," edited by I.C. Jarvie and Nicholas Pronay.

Winston, Brian. *Claiming the Real: The Griersonian Documentary and Its Legitimations*. London: British Film Institute, 1995.

Index

Printed in March 2005
at Marc Veilleux imprimeur,
Boucherville (Québec).